# An A-Z Guide for Character Healthy Homeschooling

*Megan Ann Scheibner*

AFTERWORD BY

## Dr. Steve Scheibner

WITH BONUS CHAPTERS BY
**Katie, Peter, Emma, Molly, Nate
Baleigh, Stephen, Taylor, and Emerson**

**An A-Z Guide For Character Healthy Homeschooling**
By Megan Ann Scheibner

Produced and Distributed by:

**Character Health Corporation**
101 Casablanca Ct.
Cary, NC 27519

Cover design by **ebook-designs.co.uk**

Printed in the United States

# Dedication

To my precious Savior, Jesus Christ: Only You could have changed
a tomboy like me into a joyful wife and mother!

And

To Steve: My best friend, hero, and husband. Your steadfast example
of courage, faith, and hard work inspires me daily.
I'm so glad you picked me!

And

To all the Scheiblets: Thanks for being my guinea pigs!
Boy, oh boy, do we have some memories!

Other Books
by Megan Ann Scheibner

*In My Seat:*
*A Pilot's Story from Sept. 10th – 11th*

*Grand Slam:*
*An Athletes Guide to Success in Life*

*Rise and Shine:*
*Recipes and Routines For Your Morning*

*Lunch and Literature*

*Dinner and Discipleship*

*Studies in Character*

*The King of Thing*
*and the Kingdom of Thingdom*

You can find these books and other resources at:
*CharacterHealth.com*

# Table of Contents

# Table of Contents

# An
# A-Z Guide
## *for*
# Character Healthy
# Homeschooling

# Foreword

The book you're about to read has been rattling around in my brain for many, many years. From the beginning of our homeschooling journey we've had other families ask us many homeschooling questions; so many, in fact, that I couldn't even begin to answer them all here. I think because our family exhibited such happiness in our homeschooling adventure, others saw our contentment and wanted to know how to achieve that same joy and laughter. I often had friends ask to come and follow us around for a few days, just to observe what we were doing during our homeschooling day. To be honest, I was never comfortable with that suggestion. Not because we had anything to hide, but because how we homeschooled wouldn't necessarily work for another family. I hesitated to have another mother burden herself with unnecessary expectations by trying to do exactly what we did, and then not having the same results. Instead, I happily shared what worked for us, what thrilled us, what discouraged us, and the various pitfalls we had made in our homeschooling journey. I encouraged my friends to seek God and pursue their own unique homeschooling experience.

Now, traveling across the country teaching parenting conferences, the questions have multiplied. I love answering those questions, and I would love to chat over coffee with all of the dear moms and dads that want to know more about our homeschooling lifestyle but that just isn't possible. Still, I hate to walk away and leave those questions unanswered. I prayed about how to solve this dilemma, and, as always, God was faithful to provide an answer.

What you hold in your hands is the written answer to so many of those questions parents ask. Disciplining myself to write it all down has truly forced me to examine our homeschooling choices. As you'll read in these pages, my heart's desire is to raise character-healthy kids; kids who love Jesus, love their family, and who make their God look great. I've tried to be transparent in my writing, and you'll see that, yes, sometimes we achieved my lofty goal, but sometimes poor decision making caused us to fall short. I hope our experiences can be a springboard for you and your family as you seek to glorify God through homeschooling. I can't tell you exactly how to run your family's homeschool, but hopefully I've provided some helpful tools to assist you in prayerfully following God's unique direction for your unique family.

Before we begin, let me introduce you to my family. At the end of the book, you'll hear from all of the children and my husband, but just to give you a sneak peek at our crew, here's our cast of crazy characters.

**Megan:** That's me! I spent my early years as a tennis-playing tomboy. Somehow, God saw fit to transform me into a wife, mother of eight awesome kids, and now an author and conference speaker. I love writing, cooking, reading, flirting with my husband of 28 years, and the Boston Red Sox. Fortunately, my dear husband never lets me down, but oh, those Red Sox….

**Steve:** My husband Steve is my hero. He began our marriage as a Navy pilot and served both actively and in the reserves for 29 years. We're proud to be a military family. He worked hard to earn two Masters degrees and a Doctorate degree. He is a commercial airline pilot, pastored for 10 years, and now runs our family ministry, Characterhealth Corporation. It makes me tired just thinking about all he does! He's silly about me and can still make me blush after all these years. Besides being the hottest date I ever had, he's my best friend and staunchest cheerleader.

**Kaitlyn Elizabeth:** Kaite is our oldest daughter. At 25, she is busy establishing her own home. After college, Kaite married her sweetheart, Mason, and she spends her days as a nanny for triplets and a single. As you'll read in the last chapter, Kaite loves to read, and she is a talented writer, quilter, and musician. Kaite lives in Maine, but we talk every day, which makes the separation easier.

**Peter Warren:** Peter is 11 months younger than his older sister. He arrived a month early and that impatience has characterized his entire life! Peter has always been eager to, "Get on with it." Peter and his dear wife Rochelle live 15 minutes from us, and Rochelle works for our ministry. Peter is our right-hand man when it comes to anything technological and even more importantly, when we need someone to wrestle with the little boys.

**Emily Marion:** Emma, as she's known, is our culinary genius. She received her degree in Culinary Science and is completing her Bachelor's degree in Business. She's been married for two years to her college sweetheart, Steve. Together, they are relocating to San Francisco where Emma will pursue her dream of mentoring under a well-known chef. Emma looks, acts, and thinks like me…sometimes I feel sorry for Steve!

**Margaret Hannah:** Molly is just about to turn 21. In fact, she'll celebrate her 21st birthday during her Air Force basic training. Yes, it was a surprise when our daughter decided to enlist, but as she's been preparing to leave we've seen God growing her up and equipping her to face this challenge. Molly is hilarious, and we all agree that someday she should host her own comedy show, ala Carol Burnett.

**Nathaniel Pierce:** Nate is our hardworking, Residential Construction major. He is organized and loves symmetry and precision. Nate works hard on everything he does, including relationships. When we moved to North Carolina, Nate stayed behind at the university, and I miss his quirky sense of humor every day!

**Baleigh Grace:** Baleigh is our athlete. She swims, runs, and plays a mean game of Knock-Out. Baleigh plays the fiddle, sings in the choir, loves children, and can't wait to pursue a career in fashion design. Sound busy? You'll read more about her busy life from her perspective in the last chapter.

**Stephen Paul, Jr.:** We couldn't have more appropriately named this child! Stephen is so much like his father that it's comical. He loves baseball, swimming, hanging out with his best friend, and Girls! (With a capital G) At 14, he's still not ashamed to snuggle with his mom, and he makes me smile every day!

**Taylor Christian:** Tate is our adopted blessing from Guatemala. His adoption was such a God-thing, and we can't imagine what our family would be like without him. He loves to serve his mom and dad and is creative in his service towards us. He and Stephen are inseparable and the older siblings dote on him ridiculously.

There you have it, the whole Scheibner crew. I hope as you read this book you'll get a picture of how God can take a large family full of distinctly different personalities and mold them into a vessel suitable for His use. None of us has arrived, and we're sure not perfect. But, I can speak for all of us when I say that we're blessed, and homeschooling has been a huge part of that blessing.

Stay strong dear homeschooling friends! Remember Galatians 6:9, "Don't grow weary of doing good, for in due time we'll reap if we do not grow weary." I'm looking forward to reaping together with you!

# Introduction

Twenty years of homeschooling...Wow! When I started this adventure in 1993, I simply couldn't have imagined what an important part an educational decision would play in developing who we are as a family unit. Homeschooling has become so much more than just something we "do" and instead has became a part of the fabric of our daily family life.

When I began homeschooling with my then two little students, I planned our schooling around a set amount of hours on a set number of days. Quickly, however, that plan changed to encompass school at all times, whenever and wherever we found ourselves at the moment. I realized that we were learning all of the time and contrived times of, "This is school, so pay attention." just didn't fit into our learning lifestyle.

So much has changed since 1993. Back then I hesitated to take my children out in town during regular government school hours. When I did venture out, inevitably we encountered the question, "Shouldn't you be in school today?" Homeschooling was unusual, and people wondered if what we were doing was legal. Record keeping and evaluations were onerous and provided a hazy background of uncertainty for many of us early homeschoolers. Would the truant officer show up on our doorstep? What if our neighbors, or in some cases, our relatives called the DHS? What if the teachers were right and we were handicapping our children's futures? Curriculum choices were sparse and extra-curricular activities were limited.

Thankfully, because of the legislative work of dedicated homeschooling parents, many of those early paradigms have virtually disappeared. Today, according to researchers at the Homeschool Legal Defense Association, there are an estimated 1,700,000 to 2,100,000 children in grades K-12 educated at home. No longer are we considered eccentric or somewhat radical oddities. No, homeschool has moved into the mainstream with a bang! Colleges now seek out homeschool applicants, delighted with their academic foundation and social maturity.

With that change in acceptability has come a shift in the entire structure of the homeschool community. Instead of meeting with a few moms to put together a craft class or a science lab, large co-ops offer classes to meet every possible homeschool need. The opportunities for learning, socializing, and growth are endless. In fact, unlike the days of searching for activities for my children to be involved in, today there is such a vast wealth of opportunities that the decision becomes how to choose what is best from the myriad of options. Instead of worrying that perhaps we aren't getting enough socialization, I find myself balancing my kids busy social calendars. I've stopped pursuing more options for them and instead fight to protect our precious family time!

Opportunities aren't limited to educational pursuits either. In the athletic realm, doors are opening wide for homeschoolers to pursue and excel at their given sport. Thanks to the positive notoriety of athletes such as Tim Tebow, many states are reconsidering their restrictive laws and welcoming homeschool students onto their teams. My own kids have participated on public school teams, and the feedback from their coaches has been very encouraging. The leadership, cooperation, and work ethic shown by homeschool athletes thrilled these coaches. Even in states where homeschool athletes are prohibited from competing on the public school teams, homeschool teams are filling the vacancy. Some of these teams are as large or larger than their Christian and public school counter-parts, and many produce athletes of the highest caliber; athletes who find themselves in great demand by college coaches. While it's still an inordinate amount of work to fill out the additional NCAA paperwork required for homeschool students, changes are taking place in that arena, as well.

All of these changes have made homeschooling easier than ever. But as always, change brings both positive and negative con-sequences. In the early years of homeschooling, I would often have conversations with other homeschoolers about the need to show Christ and His excellence through our homes and homeschooling. We were all very aware that our families, friends, and neighbors were watching us closely to see how this experiment of homeschooling would work out. Such scrutiny from others was a great outward motivator to make sure that we were training children who would shine in their testimonies while excelling in their academics.

The now commonplace nature of homeschooling has changed that paradigm somewhat. More and more I talk with homeschool-ing parents who are very concerned that their children have the same opportunities as the government school children. They want their children to fit in and to merge seamlessly with everyone in the youth group, neighborhood, or athletic team. Socialization isn't an issue anymore, but neither, necessarily, are Biblical character-driven standards. Because homeschooling has become so mainstream, more and more families are choosing to homeschool because of the opportunity for advanced educational pursuits, or because they can focus more exclusively on music, or art, or...you can fill in the blank. Because they are not homeschooling from a Biblical perspective, the idea of using their homeschool to develop Biblical character is foreign to them.

With this shift in the homeschooling paradigm is coming a shift in the perception of homeschoolers. Christian homeschoolers are not standing out as different, as lights in a lost world, but instead are being lumped with homeschoolers in general, and homeschoolers in general, whether Christian or not, are losing their reputation for excellent character and courageous leadership. Yes, we're excelling in academics and on the athletic fields, but we're losing our drive to excel in the character arena. We're fitting in, and that's to our detriment.

So, what's the answer? Should we forsake all the wonderful opportunities afforded to our children and hunker down in our family fortress? Should we quit the teams and drop out of the enrichment classes? No, I don't think so! Instead, we need to reaffirm in our individual families the desire to honor God through and with our homeschooling. We need to make the teaching of character paramount in our choices of activities, educational resources, and affiliations. We need to purpose in our hearts to train a new generation of Christ-like, character-healthy leaders. If we will commit to raising character champions, the other areas of our children's lives will easily fall into place. Important character qualities such as: persistence, diligence, self-control, honesty, courage, commitment, and a hard work ethic will provide them with the foundation to excel in academics, extra-curricular activities, and relationships.

Do you remember why you first chose homeschooling? Didn't you want your children to stand out as loving leaders committed to serving one another and their God? Don't lose sight of that goal. Don't let the world distract you from the main focus of your homeschool: instilling your values in your children.

We must put first things first, and Biblical character must be that first thing! It isn't hard, but it does take hard work. Will you join me in raising a new breed of young adults; young adults who love God, consistently make character healthy decisions, and who will raise the standard for generations to come! Together, we can help our young homeschooled adults build a legacy of honor, courage, and most of all, character.

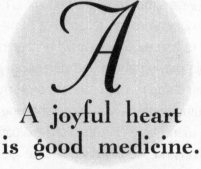

## A joyful heart is good medicine.

Proverbs 17:22

# Attitude is Everything

When it comes to homeschooling, our attitude and our children's attitudes should be our number one priority. So it is only fitting that the letter "A" and the word "Attitude" become our starting point for this primer. Although we may be able to complete the assigned curriculum for a year, and although we may dutifully check off all of our necessary days to fulfill the requirements for a year of homeschooling, if the attitudes in our home are lacking character, we have accomplished nothing of lasting value. Attitude and the subsequent character qualities that flow from a Christ-like attitude are the foundation on which a character-healthy homeschool is constructed. Without positive attitudes our homeschools run the risk of becoming battlegrounds with child pitted against child or all of the children allied against mom and dad.

Let's begin with our attitudes, mom and dad. If our attitude is negative or "Oh, woe is me" about the upcoming homeschool year, we can expect our children to reflect that same attitude. Before ever beginning to homeschool, I would encourage you to spend time as a couple praying about and discussing your decision to homeschool your children. If you cannot homeschool with a positive, pleasant attitude, why are you homeschooling at all? For single moms or dads, spend time with the Lord evaluating your homeschooling decision and seeking His guidance. God is the perfect Father to your children, and He can infuse you with the peace and courage that you will need to complete the homeschooling task you are beginning. Once we have made the decision to homeschool, our attitudes need to reflect peace and steadfastness in that decision. A continual wavering or nervous "I hope we're doing the right thing" attitude will only cause our children to worry and feel insecure about your decision to homeschool them.

Yes, homeschooling is hard work at times, but nothing worthwhile comes about without hard work. When our focus is on the work, our attitude will reflect that focus. Those are the days that I just can't seem to find any joy in homeschooling and when every wrong answer or poorly written sentence makes me irritable and crabby. On those days it seems as though my children are out to get me, and their every mistake is directly aimed at causing me heartache. That response isn't my children's fault. It is my own, self-centered attitude and a lack of character-healthy decision making. If I want my children to embrace homeschooling as the best choice for our family, I must show them through my attitude that I believe it is the best choice as well.

What kind of attitudes should our children see in our lives? As well as seeing peace and steadfastness in our decision to homeschool, I believe our children should see a clearly evident attitude of thankfulness. I don't know about you, but I'm very thankful for the opportunity to homeschool my children. Regardless of the busyness involved in having eight children at home with me all day, I can look back at our years of homeschooling and see how clearly God has blessed that decision. I want my children to know, without a doubt, that I am thankful to spend my days with them. I can show them that thankfulness through a grateful attitude and through abundant words of thankfulness. "I'm so glad I get to be with you guys!" can go far in changing the complexion of a less-than stellar day.

When we are going through difficult or trying seasons of homeschooling in our family, my husband will often ask me to tell him three things for which I'm thankful. He never lets me get away with backhanded complaints like, "The children didn't dawdle as much as usual." either! Forcing myself to stop and consider what I have to be thankful for is a powerful antidote to a negative and complaining spirit. Sometimes I ask my children the same question. As they recite their answers, we are all reminded of the goodness of God toward our family and of the myriad ways He has blessed, protected, and nurtured us.

I want my children to know that I find great joy in spending my days with them! By nature, I have a somewhat melancholy personality. No, let me be honest, by nature I'm a very melancholy personality! Although years of ministry have taught me to laugh and be pleasant for the sake of others, when I am left to my own devices, I will quickly become like Eeyore. "Oh woe is me…." For my children to realize that I am finding joy in our days, I must make the extra effort to let that joy show on my face. I'm afraid that there are some days that my children probably assume that I'm just miserable being at home with them. I'm not! Those are the days that I just haven't taken the time to let my inner joy show on the outside. My children need to see that joy or soon they will begin to feel like a burden and an unwelcome intrusion in my day. Sometimes I need the reminder, "If you're happy and you know it then your face will surely show it!" I can exhibit joy to my children by stopping to sing silly songs with them or by doing something totally unexpected. When they see mom is happy, my children are freer to be happy also.

One final but extremely important attitude, or character quality, for parents is an attitude of perseverance. There are days that because of outside activities, or illness, or conflict, or laziness, etc. that homeschooling just doesn't flow easily. On those days, it is my attitude of perseverance that will encourage my children to keep on trying. If I allow myself to embrace a quitter's attitude, my children will feel free to embrace such an attitude as well. Our family motto is: "We are the Scheibners, who never give up!" If I'm not careful, I can unwittingly change that motto to: "We are the Scheibners, who quit when it's hard…or boring…or when we find something better to do!"

What about the children? I can control (or at least try to control) my own attitude, but it is not as easy to control my children's attitudes. Although I can't change my children's attitudes for them (sure wish I could!), I can teach and train them to recognize what attitudes are acceptable and what attitudes bring harm and discord into our homeschooling. Then, I can hold them accountable to maintain good attitudes and to show those good attitudes through their character-healthy choices.

Before my children will ever be able to show good attitudes in our homeschooling, I must be diligently teaching them to exhibit good attitudes in our home and family. Homeschooling is not a stand-alone time requiring better attitudes than family time; rather, it is simply an extension of our family and our family's standard for attitudes. The foundation of good attitudes in our children is found in their response to us and to our reasonable requests. Children who are characterized by first-time obedience will have a much easier time responding to their parents when mom and dad are not just mom or dad but "teacher" as well.

To help our children develop an attitude of first-time obedience, we incorporated a simple acronym- RAH. When I say "RAH!" to my children they immediately know what I expect of them, and they are able to be successful in obedience. R stands for "Right Away." From the beginning we taught our children to obey us right away. Besides showing respect for authority, immediate obedience is a safeguard for our children. There are times that to NOT obey us immediately could mean permanent and devastating consequences for our children. Obeying right away is a protection from harm. Also, immediate obedience to us builds a strong habit of obedience that can then transfer to immediate obedience to the Lord. When the Lord calls, I want my children to be ready to do whatever He asks, whenever He asks, and to go wherever He wills.

The letter A in RAH stands for "All the Way." Until our children's obedience is "all the way," it is incomplete. Incomplete obedience builds hard-to-break habits of work poorly done and instructions poorly followed. Work hard to teach your children to follow through completely on whatever is being asked of them. Your diligent training now will have positive consequences when they are older. Remember, work that is not inspected or checked on will quickly become work that is incomplete or simply left undone. Until our children are characterized by a strong work ethic and a faithful completer's attitude, they need us to oversee their efforts. Yes, it's work to follow-up on our children's chores and academics, but the pay-off will be sweet when they are eagerly sought in the workplace because of their great finisher's attitudes.

Finally, the H in RAH stands for "The Happy Way." We train our children to obey with a happy, joyful attitude. Although what they are being asked to do might not be thrilling, obeying with a proper attitude can produce joy in their hearts. Grumpy, unhappy children, who do what they are asked with an unpleasant or scowling countenance, may be obeying on the outside, but in their heart they are holding on to a disobedient and joyless attitude. Watch your children's attitude in obedience and help them learn to obey you happily. Your example of happiness as you obey the Lord or the other lawful authorities in your life will become your strongest teaching tool. Conversely if you have a grumbling or discordant attitude when it comes to obedience, you can expect your children to inherit that attitude as well. I'm fairly sure that sometimes my attitude toward the Lord is along the lines of, "You're not the boss of me!" Is it any wonder that my little children try to show me that same attitude, complete with hands on the hips and a toss of the head?

Once our children learn to consistently obey us Right Away, All the Way, and the Happy Way in their normal daily lives, transferring that attitude to homeschooling will be an easy task. Our children will already possess the tools they need to exhibit a great attitude, even on the most difficult homeschooling day. Now, that doesn't mean that you'll never have a day made difficult by inappropriate attitudes. Our homeschools are made up of young sinners being instructed by an older sinner, so attitude problems will sometimes rear their ugly heads. However, understanding how to obey with proper attitudes will go far in helping our children to push the reset button on those off days. Did I say our children? Knowing how to obey God with a proper attitude will help US to push the reset button on our ugly days, too!

Think about the poor attitudes you deal with in your homeschooling; attitudes such as laziness, argumentative spirits, and grumbling can all be dealt with by the simple reminder to obey

Right Away, All the Way, the Happy Way. Take the time to teach your children this important concept. Remind them that their attitude about you, their schoolwork, and homeschooling in general, is much more important to you than the actual amount of work they get accomplished. In fact, we believed so strongly that character and attitude were the most important aspect of our homeschooling that we would call a halt to book learning for as long as necessary to deal with yucky attitudes. (More about that later.)

Attitude is everything! Without a character-healthy attitude in place, we run the risk of training highly educated, but character-starved children. Define your family's standard for attitude, set the example yourself, and hold your children accountable to exhibit Christlike attitudes throughout their day.

And to make it your ambition to lead
a quiet life and attend to your own
business and work with your hands,
just as we commanded you.

I Thessalonians 4:11

# Balance, Balance, Balance

Homeschooling and learning new things together with my children can be addictive. There are times that I find it hard to stop our academic studies in order to move on to the other necessary parts of our lives. However, even though it is tempting to squeeze in one more lesson or one more activity into our day, it is important to practice balance in our homeschooling.

Certainly academics are important, but to truly develop character-healthy children we must make sure that they are developing their whole self: their minds, their bodies, and their spirits. How can we develop all three areas in a well-balanced way? As with any other part of homeschooling, it takes consistency and self-discipline on our part to make sure that our children are not imbalanced in one direction or another.

Along with consistent time spent on their academics, our children need to spend time building strong bodies. Strong bodies will help them be less likely to catch every germ they encounter, and more importantly, strong bodies will equip them to be available and able to complete any task the Lord assigns to them. It has been my observation over the last 20 years of homeschooling, that homeschoolers as a whole are becoming more and more sedentary. Instead of spending time pursuing sports or outdoor activities, homeschoolers seem to be finding their enjoyment in extra reading time or in some type of technology. This lack of physical activity is an imbalance in the life of a child. Honestly, this lifestyle is an imbalance for us as well. Healthy, fit moms and dads will not only set the example for their children but will also enjoy more energy to keep up with their little powerhouses!

Find an activity that your child enjoys and encourage their participation. I tried to encourage my children to experiment with different types of outdoor activities and sports. Although I didn't insist that they stick with a sport or activity if they didn't enjoy it, I did require them to finish whatever season they began. Then, if they still didn't like what they had chosen, I allowed them to switch to another activity. Not allowing our children to just quit when they are disinterested, disappointed, or just no longer excited about a sport, teaches the important character qualities of commitment and loyalty to their team. Even at the times that my children have ended up sitting on the bench for most of the season, God has had important lessons to teach them about teamwork and being happy for others. I must be honest here and share that those seasons spent on the bench were important learning times for me as well. During a busy sports season when I was driving here and there to get my children to their chosen activities, to see a child simply sitting on the bench for most of the game sometimes seemed like a terrible waste of my time. Thankfully, my husband always helped me to keep my eye on the goal…character-building. Even when a son or daughter wasn't experiencing much playing time, they were learning how to support others, cheer for their friends, and to still work hard even when the result wasn't what they had hoped. Character isn't only built on the field; it's built during practice, on the sideline, and even on the bench.

For some children, spending time being physically active is no problem. They long to be outside, and when they have the choice they will willingly leave their books and race outside to get some physical exercise. Other children, however, are more likely to stay inside and spend their free time reading or using the computer. Regardless of their preferred activity, it is still important to encourage them to work on building their physical muscles in the same way that they build their mental muscles. Keep trying until you find something they can enjoy. If necessary, put limits on their technology use and insist that they find a physical activity to get involved with instead.

In our home, we have limited our children's Wii playing to the "Wiikends." Knowing that playing games on the Wii is not an option during the week has forced my less active children to get up and find other activities in which to be involved. Outside activities don't necessarily have to involve playing sports. My second son has discovered a love for working in the yard and landscaping. Although he is by nature a more sedentary child, he has learned to force himself to go outside and work. The more he has disciplined himself to build this habit, the more he has grown to love puttering in the yard. At this writing, he is working diligently to build a rock wall along the perimeter of our property. This is dirty, backbreaking labor, but it is paying great physical benefits in Nate's life. Our yard looks fantastic, too, which is a wonderful benefit to me!

Along with balancing the mental and physical wellbeing of our children, we must carefully equip the spiritual health of our children. We do this as we naturally incorporate spiritual teaching throughout our days. Family devotions, scripture memorization, and times of prayer are all foundational in developing our children's spiritual health. However, without putting what they are learning into practice, we run the risk of raising very "heady" Christians, who have no heart for the lost or true commitment to being a submitted servant of Christ. I believe the best way to reach the goal of helping our children to internalize the spiritual lessons we are imparting to them is by balancing service to others with academics. As our children serve others they will be building spiritual and character muscles that will prepare them to be leaders with their friends, in their churches, and in their communities. They will be putting flesh on the concepts that they have already learned through our family discussions and church involvement.

I love serving alongside my children! For years we spent our Monday mornings driving to a nearby Christian camp and cleaning their bathrooms. After weekends filled with young campers the bathrooms were a mess, and the work was often dirty and somewhat disgusting. My children learned such important lessons as we scrubbed those bathrooms together. They learned that every job they did needed to be done excellently. It wasn't good enough to just clean up the messes left behind; we needed to make those bathrooms shine! As we worked together scrubbing toilets, polishing mirrors, and mopping floors, we discussed how even a clean bathroom could be a part of winning an unsaved person to the Lord. We talked about how every area of the camp needed to show the excellence of the Savior.

Those bathroom discussions opened wide the door to discussions about the need to show the excellence of Christ in every area of our own lives. We were able to talk about how the sins and poor character that we allowed to remain in our lives could distract people from seeing just how great our God was and how much they needed Him too. As we polished mirror after mirror, we discussed how to become a clear reflection of our shining God. After working hard serving together, I would always notice just how relaxed and peaceful my children became. They would easily talk and discuss spiritual topics with no defensiveness or excuse making.

It is important to teach our children to serve in the unglamorous and unexciting areas of life. Something I have observed about homeschoolers, and I include myself in this assessment, is our desire to have our children serve up front, where they will be recognized and rewarded. It is imperative that our children learn to serve faithfully behind the scenes before they become addicted to serving publicly and only when there is some sort of recognition.

When the bulk of our children's serving is in public, or publicly recognized, we run the risk of developing a haughty or selective attitude in our children. Instead of serving wherever and whenever they are needed, they will limit themselves to "applaudable" service. I don't know about you, but I sure wouldn't want to be married to someone who only served when there was applause or recognition involved in the service. How we train our children now will build the habits that characterize their lives as husbands and wives when they are grown. Today's choices will either help them to build a heart and attitude that loves to serve, or their choices will facilitate the development of a heart and attitude that longs instead to be served. Little choices we make today are so important for tomorrow. We must teach our children to be humble and willing servants; willing to do whatever is needed without first asking, "What's in it for me?"

As always, your balance in all these areas of life will be the example that speaks to your children's hearts. Are you growing and learning mentally? Do you take care of your physical wellbeing in order to be an available and hard worker? Are you characterized by serving others, even if that serving has no immediate benefit for you? If one area or another is out of whack, pray and make a plan to bring your life into a healthy, God-honoring balance. Be transparent and share your own struggles in these areas with your children. As you pray together about developing a well-balanced life, mentally, physically, and emotionally, your whole family will be building a lasting legacy and testimony for the Lord.

# *C*

O clap your hands,
all peoples; Shout to God
with the voice of joy.

Psalm 47:1

# Contagious
Excitement

Once upon a time, a brand new Christian named Megan joined a ministry to high school students. Megan was a 19 year-old college student, and if she knew anything, she knew how important it was to be cool. Imagine her shock and dismay when at her first ministry event she was dressed in overalls, had hay stuck in her hair, and was instructed to recite a poem titled "Moose Goosers." And that wasn't the end of it! The next week she was dressed up again and recited "Cow Tippers," then "Deer Lickers," and the list went on. What in the world was going on?

I'm that girl, and my introduction into ministry was preparing me, although I didn't realize it at the time, to be Rah-Rah-Sis-Boom-Bah cheerleader for our family homeschool. When I began to work as a Young Life leader, the staff folks taught me an important lesson.

While I thought it was important for me to exude cool in order to get kids to like me and want to join the Young Life group, the truth was those same kids just wanted to know if I was excited. Was I excited about them? Was I excited about ministry? Ultimately, was I excited about the Lord? I soon learned that to generate excitement with the teens, I couldn't just be sort of excited. No, I needed to be ten times as excited as they were. You know what? As I "forced" myself to exude excitement, I actually became excited! The more excited I was about the ministry and ministry activities, the more excited the kids became as well. Suddenly, "cool" took on a whole new definition in my life.

Fast-forward twelve years to the beginning of the Scheibner Family Homeschool. My children, who up until that time had enjoyed massive amounts of free time, were a bit skeptical about this new homeschool arrangement. That's when my Young Life training kicked into gear. I wasn't sure what homeschooling was going to look like exactly. I wasn't sure how the whole adventure was going to work out, but I did know how to be excited. As I began homeschooling my children, I exuded over the top excitement about what we, as a family, were privileged to do. Not so easy for an Eeyore like me, but I realized how important my level of excitement was for motivating my children. As I prayed and asked the Lord to help me encourage the children's excitement, He was faithful to fill me with excitement as well. Pretty soon, just like before, the excitement wasn't a put-on. Every day I became more excited about what we were learning and about the time I was able to spend with my children. I was excited about the service opportunities we were finding. I was excited about the ability we had to practice hospitality as a family. Excitement about homeschooling my children had become the norm for my life.

When you have eight children in one home, everything gets

shared. From shoes, to shirts, to books...we pass them on. The sharing syndrome is especially true when my children catch a flu bug. We're just a science experiment waiting to happen! I can't think of a single time that one child got sick without everyone else catching the bug as well. Large families are just contagious like that. So it is with excitement. When we are excited about our homeschooling, our children will be excited as well. When I began to bubble over with excitement each day, so did my children. When we are lethargic and apathetic about our homeschooling, our children will be lethargic and apathetic as well. On the days I just don't feel like homeschooling, my children don't want to participate in homeschooling any more than I do. My excitement, or lack thereof, becomes the catalyst for the attitudes within our home.

What things can you be excited about in your homeschooling situation? The things that come immediately to mind for me are these: unlimited time with my children, seeing them learn (especially when they learn to read by themselves), field trips, exploring together, baking together, watching them build lifelong relationships and close friendships with one another, spending time opening our home together. Your list may not look like mine, but I am sure that there are unique qualities about your homeschool that make homeschooling exciting for you.

Now that you've thought about what excites you in homeschooling, it's time to let that excitement show! There is something very "adultish" about being cool. If we want our children to be excited about learning, and especially about learning at home, we need to discard our cool attitudes and be the Head Cheerleader for our family homeschool. Don't worry about looking foolish. Foolish to us is endearing to our children.

Look for ways to find excitement throughout the day. We live in the woods and often have critters wander into the yard. Because

I am by nature a task-oriented, "Must get it done" mother, my first inclination is to see the animal, register its existence in my mind, think, "I don't want the kids to stop what they're doing," and then go on about my day. As the cheerleader for excitement in our home I needed to change my natural inclinations! Now, when I see some critter encroaching on my property I start the "Come and see!" cheer. The children and I gather in the window, and we watch the animals graze, or dig, or burrow, or whatever other destruction they are bringing to my yard. We laugh together at the turkeys and whisper so as not to frighten the deer. We bob our head in rhythm with the woodpecker. We enjoy the moment together.

When I bake bread, I often call the younger children over to watch the yeast ferment. Besides being a quick science lesson, it is fun to watch the bubbles expand and burst, and the 3-minute break from their schoolwork builds memories. When I run the blender, all of the children join hands and form a chain from the blender, to me, and on down the line. Once the blender starts running that whole silly chain starts jiggling and gyrating. When their dad is home he looks at us like we've all lost our minds, but occasionally we've been able to guilt him into joining our Blender Congo Line! None of these things take much time, but they make our days fun and laughter-filled.

Just an encouragement for those of you with large families…. Several years ago I began to notice that many of the fun memories that the children were sharing were foreign to the youngest children. While the older kids had great memories of trips to the zoo and mornings spent apple picking, the busyness of life and heavier academic load of my older students had brought an end to many of our favorite activities. Although in some ways my younger children exhibited more maturity than their older siblings had at the same age, they had also missed some really fun "younger" kid activities.

After realizing this paradigm, I began to make it a point to re-incorporate more of the younger, kid-friendly activities. I reminded the older children of their fond memories of such times and recruited their help to make building memories with the younger kids a top priority. Even activities that seemed too little-kid-like became fun for the older children as they introduced their younger siblings to the places and memories that they had already enjoyed. Teaching your older children to embrace having fun at a younger kid level is great training for parenting. I never had younger siblings, or even younger cousins, and it was a steep learning curve for me to understand how to play and explore with my little ones. Obviously, because of their extra school workload, there were times that the older kids stayed behind to study while I took off with the younger children, but as much as possible, we tried to explore and build memories together as a family.

What can you do to bring excitement to otherwise humdrum school days? Perhaps your family needs a family cheer or a family song. Be creative, relax, and enjoy your homeschool. The very things that we think are the "cheesiest" are the things that our children will remember for years. Now when my older children come home to visit, they lay around the living room talking and laughing about the silly stuff that mom did to make their days more exciting. I secretly delight in every eye roll and "Oh, mom!"

I honestly believe that our family homeschool is the neatest place on earth. When I validate that belief for my children through my excitement and creativity, I free them up to show their excitement as well. Excitement is contagious. Who have you shared the excitement germ with today?

You will surely wear out,
both yourself and these people
who are with you, for the task
is too heavy for you;
you cannot do it alone.

Exodus 18:18

# Designate Chores and Chore Time

I hate to admit this, but sometimes I think longingly of the freedom my public school friends possess. I think of the five hours a day that their houses stay clean. I daydream about my own home staying clean for that long. Fortunately, I have God's Word to cut short my reverie. It was God who called our family to this homeschooling adventure, and it is God who brings an end to my wistful daydreaming. Proverbs 14:4 reminds me of this simple truth: "Where no oxen are, the manger is clean. But much revenue comes by the strength of the ox."

It's not very complimentary, but my children are my oxen; and, just like oxen cause a mess in the manger, my children cause mess-

21

es in my home. However, as the scripture says, those same oxen will produce much revenue, or increase, in my life. My children and their godly character have strengthened and validated my husband's and my testimonies. That alone is certainly worth a messy manger!

Here's the good news. Although my oxen (children) make a messy manger, I also have them home all day to learn how to clean up their own messes! I'd like to see a farmer teach his oxen to do that! Manger management is an important part of our homeschool character-building curriculum. Training my children to faithfully execute their assigned chores teaches them faithfulness, diligence, attention to detail, responsibility, and countless other character qualities. I don't require my children to assume the responsibility of chores just so that I have less to do, although I'm sure sometimes they think that is my motivation. In fact, when I was growing up, I was absolutely convinced that my parents had adopted me just to have someone to do the dishes! Rather, I insist on chores to help them develop the skills they will need to function as well-balanced adults and to make sure that our home and homeschool operate in a decent and orderly manner.

Growing up as the youngest child in a fairly unorganized home gave me no preparation for marriage, parenting, and home management. I don't want my children to face the same hurdles I struggled so much to jump over. Learning to cook, clean, do laundry, pay bills, etc. after I was already married caused some unnecessary strife and a fairly high level of stress. If I have anything to say about it, my children will be 100% better prepared to deal with those types of responsibilities when they leave our home than I was as a young adult.

What chores do you require of your children? Kids can do so much more than we think they can do! I have found that the more important to the wellbeing of our home a chore is, the more carefully a child attends to that chore. Our kids know when a chore is just busy work. Make sure that the jobs you are asking them to complete on a regular basis are jobs that will benefit the family unit as a whole.

What jobs fall into the children's chore category? Here are some of the chores my kids have taken responsibility to fulfill: cooking, laundry, yard work, cleaning the bathrooms, emptying the trash, cleaning out cars, vacuuming carpets, mopping wood and linoleum floors, washing dishes, babysitting siblings, and once they get their license, chauffeur duty. One of my sons tells all his friends that once he received his driver's license "we" suddenly became a synonym for "you." As in, "We need to pick up some milk at the store. Here are the car keys!"

Obviously, my children haven't done all of those chores at the same time, but all of the children have learned to complete all of the chores. Also, as you can see from my list, some chores are more desirable than others. Regardless of the desirability of a chore, it is important for our children to learn competence, even in strongly disliked jobs.

I have tried many different types of chore systems. We've used charts, reminder cards, sticky notes, drawing a chore out of a basket, and verbal assignments. What has worked best for us, and this has been our system for six years now, is to assign a major yearly chore to each child with other chores verbally assigned on an "as needed" basis. At the beginning of each school year, I designate the new chore for the year. Whoever had the chore the year before is responsible to train the new owner of the chore. For the first couple of weeks I supervise the learning process, and I spot check periodically. During the training process I make sure that the children understand exactly what I expect from them. For example, being assigned the chore of keeping the floors clean doesn't simply mean running the vacuum cleaner. Clean floors involve broom sweeping, periodic mopping, etc. Laying out the standard ahead of time saves heartache later and gives our children the opportunity to succeed and even to excel.

I recently read a quote that really made sense to me. It said, "You can't expect what you don't inspect." Isn't that the truth?! If I just send my children off every day to complete their chores with no type of inspection or accountability, what I can expect is work poorly done. Spot checks and periodic inspections keep our kids accountable to do their work excellently. As well, generously praising our children for a job well done will cause them to work harder and look forward to displaying their completed jobs for our inspection.

Having a set time to complete chores will help your children develop a routine and habit of getting their work done. For our family, chore time is immediately after breakfast. While the children are getting their chores done, I have time to complete preparations for the day and get any meal prep started. Occasionally, one of the little boys will wake up early and get his chore done before breakfast, but that's the exception not the norm.

Certain jobs are more desirable than others, but since everyone knows that their chore will only last for one year, I don't deal with too much grumbling. I will, however, make an exception to the one-year rule. If a child spends the entire year doing the chore poorly, with no noticeable effort put into improving their quality of workmanship, I will re-assign the same chore for a second year. That has only happened once, to one child, and their consequence seems to have served as a deterrent to the other children. That dynamic is one of the greatest benefits of family peer pressure!

Chores don't have to be a dismal time of hard labor. Often, I turn on the CD player and we dance around the house as we complete our chores. Sometimes, if I know a certain child is going to have a particularly difficult or busy day, I will help them with their chore or even step in to do the chore in their place for that day. Seeing me willing to complete their chore for them on a hard day has produced great character fruit, as many times I've seen those same children step in to help a busy brother or sister.

Besides assigned chores, my children know that they are all responsible to keep their rooms clean. Messy rooms are not a right that our children possess. We often remind the children that their rooms belong to us, and they are simply occupying our space. Therefore, our standard of cleanliness is the standard that needs to be upheld.

My youngest daughter, Baleigh, seems to have the hardest time managing her room. She is an extremely busy seventeen year-old and often her room becomes nothing more than a pit stop between activities. As well, she is a "collector" and finds it difficult to throw anything out. I realized that Baleigh and I were beginning to have frequent disagreements about her room. Often, what she considered clean and what I considered clean were two very different standards. I prayed about a solution, and this is what the Lord impressed on my heart.

One afternoon, I told Baleigh that she and I would be working together in her room. I assured her that I wasn't going to get angry with any messes we uncovered, but that we were going to work together to develop a system to keep her room clean and organized. Armed with garbage bags, baskets, and storage containers, we tackled the room. I helped Baleigh discard worn out and outgrown clothing. Then we refilled her drawers neatly. I provided a memory box for keepsakes and instructed her that she could only keep as many as would fit in the box. She sorted through her possessions and made her decisions. We threw out trash, washed mirrors, and dusted the now empty surfaces. We discussed that any new keepsakes would have to fit in the memory box, necessitating her throwing out something old to keep something new. She was thrilled with the clean and organized room and, because we worked together, the task hadn't been so daunting.

Next, came the most important step in the process. We took pictures of every area of her room. We photographed each drawer, each shelf, and under the bed. Then we hung the pictures on her bulletin board. Now when I send Baleigh to clean her room, I direct her to the pictures, which provide a visual reminder of what we expect her room to look like when she is finished cleaning. Those pictures have taken away the "bad guy" badge I was wearing and replaced it with me as a neutral mediator simply enforcing the family standard. Our relationship has improved, and Baleigh is learning important skills that she will use as a wife and mother someday.

Bedroom chores have often been a way for my children to be a blessing to one another. Sometimes I will find a sibling cleaning another sibling's room simply because they know their brother or sister is having a hard day and could use a helping hand. Those acts of loving service are a blessing to the overwhelmed child and a thrill to my heart. Occasionally they've even cleaned my room when they knew that ministry responsibilities were making me feel pressed for time to get everything done. What a treat to come home to a sparkling clean room and freshly laundered sheets! Sadly, they've occasionally used those freshly laundered sheets to "short-sheet" my bed. That's okay, I definitely know how to get even!

I know that often it is quicker and easier for you to complete the necessary jobs in your home. DON'T DO IT! You will be robbing your children of important character-building lessons. Instead, work alongside your children to teach them how to complete their assigned chores. Then step back and allow them to run with their own responsibilities. Inspect regularly and smile as you see your children embracing their part of maintaining your family's "manger."

# Through presumption comes nothing but strife.

Proverbs 13:10

# Expectations: Never Worth the Trouble They Cause!

I f one word were used to describe the cause of most of the problems we encounter in our homeschooling, the word would be: Expectations. Whether it's my expectations, my husband's expectations, or the expectations of my children, those nasty expectations stir up trouble and cause misunderstanding and conflict.

Expectations are totally different from standards. Standards are well established, well communicated ways of living for our family. We have standards concerning clothing, television viewing, friendships, music choices, and more. We try hard to make sure that our standards are Biblically based and well enforced. Expectations, on the other hand, are not well established, rarely communicated, and capricious in their enforcement.

That is not to say that expectations are necessarily wrong in and of themselves. Rather, the problem is in the lack of communication surrounding our expectations. Where standards are well thought out and established, expectations can crop up in the blink of an eye. When that happens, our children have little opportunity for success and often end up in trouble with no idea how they got there! Expectations run amuck can cause irreparable damage to family relationships.

Proverbs 13:10 states, "Through presumption comes nothing but strife." Presumption is just another word for expectation, and this verse lays out clearly the fruit of presumption...strife. When my home or homeschool seems to be overflowing with strife, often upon contemplation, I can trace the strife back to one primary source, unmet expectations. If I want to eradicate unnecessary strife from our home, and I do, I must learn to manage my own expectations and teach my children to recognize and dismiss their inappropriate expectations as well.

Managing expectations is always harder than I think it will be. In any given day I have so many unspoken expectations or assumptions for my children. I assume they just know that I want them to dress nicely because we're going out, but I don't tell them the plan of the day. I assume they know that a television show is off limits, but I don't communicate that clearly. I assume they know I'm tired, and that it isn't a good time to ask me questions. When I am filled with expectations, I am expecting my children to either read my mind or to think and process information like adults. Sometimes, I just need to remember that they are children.

The simplest antidote for dealing with expectations is a commitment to clear communication and unambiguous instructions. When I ask my children a question but I intended to give them a command, I am setting them up to fail. However, when I am clear in communicating my desires not only do they have the opportunity to succeed, I can also be confident that if they don't obey it is disobedience, not misunderstanding. I have learned to say what I mean and mean what I say with my children. I have also learned not to tack the expression, "Okay?" on the end of my directions. "Okay?" communicates a choice to my children, yet then when they act on that choice, I often harshly respond in frustration or anger. Naturally, this causes confusion for the children who thought I was giving them an option.

Expectations come to a head in our children's teen years. Too often, I find myself in a pointless disagreement with my children, simply because I feel like they have disappointed me, when actually they have just neglected to fulfill my unspoken expectations. The only solution to these fruitless arguments is to stop and seek my children's forgiveness for my lack of clear communication.

Of course sometimes it is our children who are casting their expectations heedlessly throughout our homes. It's important to teach our children how to recognize their own expectations and how to seek forgiveness when those expectations have caused strife and discord.

Is there a high level of strife in your home? Take a moment to step back and evaluate your quality of communication. Do other family members know exactly what is expected of them, or do you just assume that they know what is required? I don't believe you can over-communicate when it comes to expectations. If after prayerful evaluation you realize that your communication has been less than clear, take the time to seek forgiveness from your children. Children are exceedingly forgiving, and they will appreciate a mom who seeks to restore a relationship with them. Spend time teaching them the damage that expectations can cause and commit together to become a family characterized by clear communication and a lack of strife-causing presumptions.

There is an appointed time
for everything. And there is
a time for every event
under heaven.

Ecclesiastes 3:1

# Fun Times

True story... All work and no play makes for dull kids. Actually, all work and no play makes for a dull mommy too! Do you remember why you chose homeschooling in the first place? Although there may be a few families that decided to homeschool simply because of the "superior academic opportunities," (Yawn!) I think most of us made the choice because we wanted to invest in close relationships with our children. Certainly, we make that investment as we guide their educations, but spending time simply having FUN is the cement that holds all the other parts of homeschooling together.

What do you do to have fun? Seriously, if we don't take the time to think about having fun with our kids, it just won't happen. Chores, academics, and outside activities are insidious time snatchers, and without forethought and planning fun can soon be lost in the shuffle. Here's a little secret: Although it can be, fun doesn't always have to be educational! It took me several years to realize that when my local public school allowed the children to play volleyball for the morning, then sent them home at lunch, and then counted that as one of their required school days, those kids were just having fun, and that was okay! That little secret freed me up to relax and make having fun a normal, and acceptable, part of our homeschool.

Do you belong to a homeschool group or are you part of a local church? Take advantage of other moms' ideas and construct a resource book to spark creativity. One year, our church provided a small pamphlet entitled 100 Fun Things to do With Your Children This Summer. Wow! Was that little pamphlet ever helpful to me. I'm a very organized and routine-oriented person, so having 100 ideas available to peruse kept me from slipping into a dull routine of "fun." You know what I mean, "Oh, roller-skating was so fun! We should go roller-skating again! Let me get out my day planner and write in, 'Roller-skating every Wednesday at 1:00.' Won't that be FUN for us?" Sadly, I have the ability to turn even fun activities into something predictable and mundane.

Fun has been a lifesaver in our homeschool on more than one occasion. We live in Maine, and although Maine has some beautiful and scenic times of the year, much of the homeschool year is gray and dreary. In the winter, the sun sets by 4:00, and it's easy to become discouraged and lethargic. When we are in the midst of a seemingly never-ending string of gray days, I often prompt the children to finish their work quickly, while I find something fun and out of our normal routine to brighten the day. Allow me to share some of our favorite fun activities.

Fast-paced card games. My kids love games like Dutch Blitz, Spot It, Uno, Skip-Bo, and this really strange game they named Slap

Hands. I don't understand that game. I always lose at that game, and my children love slapping my hands as hard as they can....The little wretches! Fast-paced card games are very useful to help my children burn off some pent up energy.

Jigsaw puzzles. During the winter months, we often have a 2000 piece puzzle out on our schoolroom table. In fact, my youngest child grew up helping with those big puzzles, skipping right past the simple toddler-type puzzles. Don't tell my kids, but I always hide one piece of the puzzle so that I can put in the last piece and be the Puzzle Queen. They still haven't figured out how I always manage to have the last piece. Maybe I'll tell them when the last one leaves home! Jigsaw puzzles do a great job teaching our children important focusing, organizing, and spatial skills. They definitely fall into the "educational fun" category.

Charades, Family Talk, and Storytelling games. My kids love to play charades. In fact, that is undoubtedly the most requested fun time activity. It's probably because they are all such melodramatic hams! Another favorite is a simple game called Family Talk. We purchased this little gem at a restaurant, but I'm sure it's available online as well. Family Talk is a stack of cards asking various questions. For example: What's your favorite color? If each family member were a dog, what kind of dog would they be? What color was your bedroom when you were growing up? What scares you the most? Some questions are simply fun or silly, while other questions cause us to think and respond transparently. Our adopted son, Taylor, especially gravitates toward this game. I think knowing our answers and sharing his own answers make him feel extra connected with the family. Storytelling is a great winding down, laying on the couch activity. I'll begin a story by introducing some characters and a simple plot. After a few moments of storytelling, I stop, and whoever is sitting next to me picks up the story and continues. Sometimes our stories go on for a long time with twists and turns and silliness all mixed together. I probably should have written down some of the stories, but in the midst of the telling I never want to be left out!

Family talent night. This fun activity takes a bit more planning, but it is well worth the effort. Tell your children ahead of time that they need to plan a talent to share. It certainly doesn't need to be a serious talent, although some of my children take talent night very seriously. Whether it's whistling, singing, or strange body contortions, it encourages everyone to share their talents and rewards them with applause and accolades! Talent night is even more fun when you invite another family, or several families, to join you in the merriment. Have everyone bring desserts, and you provide the drinks. My children have had some of their greatest belly laughs watching the adults they thought were so serious dancing like Elvis or playing Amazing Grace through their nose!

Similar to talent night, but with a slightly different twist, was the Scheibner Academy Awards. From a young age our son, Peter, enjoyed making films. One year we expanded his filmmaking to include everyone in the family. For a month, different sibling groups and individuals worked to produce their own unique three-minute films. The night before our Academy Awards, we had a showing of all the films along with secret balloting to choose winners in many areas. The next night, the whole family dressed to the hilt. The girls wore heels and my old prom dresses, and the boys dressed up also, complete with duct tape ties and vests. We all took turns reading presentation speeches that we had written during the day. Even our oldest daughter called in from college and presented an award over the speakerphone. We had winners for Best Actress, Best Actor, Best Screenplay, Costume Design, Best Special Effects, you name it we covered every category! Basically, everyone received an award and then gave an acceptance speech into Mr. Microphone.

Everyone that is, but me; there was no award for proofreading, so I walked away empty-handed. (I'm not bitter. Honest!) What a blast, and what a great memory!

Really, that's what fun times in our homeschooling are all about…building memories. I don't believe our children will look back and remember how many math pages they completed or how many capitals they memorized; but they will remember the fun times we had as a family. Sometimes taking the time to plan fun events seems overwhelming or "just one more thing to do." Take the time to do it anyway! Even when I'm bone-tired and think I can't do one more thing, our fun times as a family have energized me and helped me get over the tiredness hump. It's well worth the effort!

What will you do for fun today? Ask your children for ideas, carve out some time, and go build some great family memories!

*G*

# But let all things be done properly and in an orderly manner.

I Corinthians 14:40

# Get Organized

Does the very word "organized" strike fear in your heart? Does it seem as though the work involved to get your home organized just isn't worth the effort? Trust me, I understand! Although some women just seem to be naturally organized and in control of their days, activities, and "stuff," for most of us, getting organized is a tedious and sometimes daunting task. However, organization can make the difference between a successful homeschooling year and a frustrating year of unfulfilled goals, unfinished projects, and incomplete learning. Even when it's difficult and time-consuming, organizing our homes and working hard to incorporate routines and habits that will help us reach our homeschooling goals, is time well- spent.

Before you jump right into organizing your home and find yourself buried in an overwhelming pile of possessions with no homes and paperwork with no systems to contain it, stop and take some time to pray about and evaluate your home's organizational needs. All homes need to be run in a decent, orderly, and organized way, but homeschooling homes are in especial need of good routines and adequate storage. Unlike homes that may stand empty for many hours of the day, our homes are filled with people and busy with activities from morning until night. The opportunities for clutter, dirt, and paper avalanches are endless. Thankfully, organized does not mean spotless or antiseptic. Rather, an organized home is a home where supplies are accessible, possessions are stewarded appropriately, and calmness and peace are the norm of the day. Although some folks may be able to function in cluttered and over-run spaces, I believe that most people, and especially children, learn best in rooms that are organized and clutter-free. Empty spaces encourage the use of imagination.

As believers, we are all instructed to practice hospitality. Does the condition of your home make you hesitant to invite others in to enjoy fellowship with your family? Our homes do not need to be large or filled with expensive furniture for us to be hospitable. In fact, some of the sweetest homes we have been invited into were very simple homes. However, these homes were characterized by their tidiness, lack of clutter, and attention to detail when it came to making guests and family members feel comfortable. Soup and bread in a cozy peaceful environment is just as enjoyable as steak in a large home when care is taken to make the home winsome and welcoming!

With paper and pencil in hand, go room to room in your home evaluating the state of each room. Are possessions put away in their proper place? Do those possessions even have a proper place? Is the room cluttered and over-run by too much "stuff"? Worse yet, is the room dirty and in need of a good scrubbing? As you answer these questions while traveling from room to room, you will begin to see an emerging picture of the actions you will need to take to get your home more organized. I have always found it helpful to make detailed lists of everything that needed to be accomplished in each room or area of my home. Although some people are comfortable working on the organization of their home slowly and over several months, I always felt like we needed to be organized before we started a new school year. Having a place for everything and everything in its place on the first day of school helped us to avoid unnecessary skirmishes over lost pencils, forgotten chores, and misplaced books. At the end of the school year, I again spent time organizing, purging, and cleaning so that we could start our summer fresh and unburdened by the clutter of a busy school year and long, gray Maine winter.

Organizing our homes to be our servants rather than our masters, involves three steps. The first step is cleaning and discarding. The second step is providing storage or containment for possessions, or what I call clutter-control. The third, and most long-term step is developing useable chore and daily touch-up routines.

Before you begin to organize your possessions into workable storage units, it is important to spend time throwing out and cleaning up. Without this first step, you will find yourself organizing "junk" that should just be discarded or given away. This is the time to be merciless on ourselves. Go through each room throwing away old toys, magazines, unraveling afghans, dead plants, etc. Keeping items like these will only make your daily routines more difficult. Sort through papers and decide which papers must be kept and which can be discarded. Generally speaking, I kept samples of my children's schoolwork from each grade level until they began their freshman year of college. I certainly didn't keep ALL of their work. Our house could never have contained it all!

As you are strategically sorting through your possessions, decide what will be thrown out, what will be given away, and what could possibly be sold at a yard sale or on the Internet. Involve your children in this process. Encourage them to donate gently used toys and craft supplies to children who may not be as blessed as them. Don't hinder their generosity. You will be amazed as you watch them joyfully preparing to give to others.

As you are purging toy boxes, drawers, and cupboards, take the time to thoroughly clean each of these areas. Don't put articles that you have decided to keep back into dirty storage areas! It is much easier to clean an empty cupboard than it is to remember to take everything out later to clean the space. Before you ever begin make sure you have all of the cleaning supplies that you will need. Nothing derails a productive day of organization like realizing that there are no paper towels or cleanser.

Don't overwhelm yourself by beginning too many areas at once. That is why lists for each room are so important. Without these lists and without a plan of attack it is easy to wander from room to room doing a little bit of this and a little bit of that, and then at the end of the day to feel like you have actually accomplished nothing! Instead, armed with your list, choose a room and begin to de-clutter and clean. Once that step is completed, put items that you plan to keep into storage containers that will work well for your family's needs. Containers don't have to be fancy or expensive, although I must admit that I love to browse through catalogs looking at all the neat ways to contain my stuff! Shoeboxes, Rubbermaid containers, empty tissue boxes, baskets, milk crates, etc. all make great storage units, and they won't break the budget.

As you organize each room, try to picture the normal flow and routine that occurs in that space. For example, when organizing the school area, consider what items are most used and make those items the most easily accessible. Find a workable way to group craft materials for your children. If they have to search all over for glue, scissors, construction paper, glitter, markers, etc., they will be much less likely to spend time creating. For our home I saved up and purchased a four-shelf jelly cupboard. Then, within that cupboard, I organized our craft materials into small see-through containers. I had one shelf for different types of paper, one shelf with crayons, markers, and colored pencils, and the other shelves held boxes of "craft starters." For example, we had boxes with small feathers, rubber stamps and inkpads, Popsicle sticks, stickers, glue sticks and rubber cement, sequins, wooden tiles, and more. Once those supplies were accessible, I watched my children's creativity flourish. I'm not a naturally "crafty" person, but my lack of creativity didn't stop my children. All they needed were supplies that had been organized for easy use and off they raced with their imaginations.

Another area of great organizational need is our kitchens. Does your kitchen function in such a way that cooking is easy and enjoyable? Or do you spend too much time searching for the measuring spoons or trying to remember which cupboard holds the muffin tins? When our kitchens are organized to work with the natural flow of our cooking, meal preparation will be less of a chore and more of a joy. Imagine that you are a stranger stepping into your kitchen to prepare a meal. Would you be able to locate all of the necessary materials easily? If not, spend some time considering how to make your kitchen work for you.

For me, organizing the kitchen into separate workspaces has been a lifesaver. I have one area for all my baking needs, i.e. flours, sugars, baking spices, measuring cups and spoons, sheet pans, cake pans, muffin tins, etc. When I want to quickly make a batch of cookies, everything is close at hand and readily accessible. Across the kitchen, I have a workspace with my cutting boards, knives, pots, and pans. When I am preparing meals, this area holds everything I need to complete my task efficiently.

As an added benefit, organizing your kitchen and making sure that the children understand the flow of organization will make it easier for them to help with kitchen clean up. Instead of finding your mixing bowls in the pantry and your measuring spoons in the silverware drawer, your children will be able to recognize where things belong, and you won't waste precious time on a scavenger hunt for your cooking tools!

As part of your kitchen organization, take some time to organize and plan your family's mealtime. A simple menu will help with food purchasing and will ensure that you have what you need when mealtime rolls around. If you're anything like me, by the end of a long day of homeschooling the last thing I want to do is decide what we're going to have for dinner. A meal plan helps me stay on top of the dinner dilemma. I can simply look at my already planned menu in the morning and know what prep work needs to be accomplished. In the same way having a plan for the kids' breakfast keeps us from filling up on cereal every day. Besides being an expensive alternative, a steady diet of sugary cereal just doesn't give my kids the energy they need for their busy days. Meal planning doesn't have to be elaborate, but in the end it always saves time, money, and frustration.

Other areas of the home will also lend themselves to specific organizational tactics. Take the time to organize DVDs, CDs, books, toys, and sports equipment. Once you have developed a good system, take the time to explain the system to your children and insist that they keep those items organized. Help them to find a natural flow of order for their own possessions. Make sure to provide storage containers for them to use for their special treasures.

Once you have organized your home in a way that works well for your whole family, make plans for how to keep it that way. Arrange your daily chores to include time spent touching up areas that tend to quickly unorganize themselves. Perhaps you could assign certain children to maintain certain areas. We had one child that took over the DVD shelf. It drove him crazy when he couldn't find the movie he wanted or when movies were put away in the wrong box, so it made sense for him to be in charge of "movie maintenance." Because my teenage daughters seem to do the most disorganizing in the bathroom cupboard, I charged them with keeping the bathroom shelves and drawers in an orderly manner. Once those areas had been initially organized, keeping up with the order wasn't difficult at all.

Learning to be organized and developing habits to maintain that organization go much further than simply ensuring a clean home and kudos from the in-laws. (Although a little praise doesn't hurt anybody!) Learning to think in an organized manner will help our children in so many other areas of life. Good test takers are often the children who have learned to look at test questions and organize the material into necessary and unnecessary facts. They can then disregard what is unnecessary and focus in on what is actually being asked. Children who have been trained to be orderly and organized will have an easier time completing their schoolwork and learning to prioritize their days. For them, organization will mean more free time to pursue their own interests.

Taking time to organize and to teach the reasons why we organize our homes will build strong character in several key areas. Our children will learn to prioritize as they discard unnecessary items. They will learn self-control as they practice the discipline of putting items where they belong instead of just throwing everything on the floor or into a closet. They will learn diligence, perseverance, and patience as they spend time maintaining the order of their rooms. I Corinthians 14:40 reminds us to do everything in a decent and orderly way. Remind your children that all of the hard work involved in organizing your home and routine isn't just about making things look better. Rather, it is the way we live out God's admonition in I Corinthians.

Speaking of priorities, it isn't only our homes that need to be organized. Just as important is the organization of our time and priorities. All of us face those days when something urgent thrusts itself into the primary position of importance. However, when we have taken the time to consider our priorities and to organize our time to meet those priorities, once the urgent is dealt with we will easily slip back into priority living. Look at your calendar. Is your time organized in such a way that the most important people and activities in your life are receiving the time and preeminence they deserve? Without an organized plan to uphold our priorities, it is easy for days, weeks, months, and even years to slip by without us noticing what we're missing. When that happens our good intentions won't replace the damage done by misplaced priorities.

I must be honest with you. This is an area that often causes me great distress, and I will beat myself up over good intentions gone unmet. Yes, there are certainly some things that I wish I had done with the older children before they left home. Sometimes those activities went uncompleted because of my laziness, but more often I didn't meet those goals because of other important activities and needs that became of primary importance. It's imperative for me to keep my eyes focused on the "big picture" of our homeschooling. We have done so many things, gone so many places, and built so many memories during our years of homeschooling. For me to dwell on what hasn't happened is to lose the perspective of the wonderful things that have been accomplished. When I slip into this attitude of guilt and regret, I become ineffective in the immediate. Instead of using my time to teach my children and build new memories, I lock myself into my past failures and disappointments. Don't get caught in the guilt trap. Make sure that you are faithfully homeschooling your children according to the Lord's direction in your life, and then relax and enjoy the adventure. Don't let guilt and self-accusation rob you from experiencing the joy of the moment!

Make living decent, orderly, and organized lives the norm in your home. Yes, it's hard work and it takes continual re-evaluation and upkeep, but the long-term fruit in your family is of great value. You will be raising sons and daughters that can begin their own families with strong, well-built habits already in place. You will be strengthening your own testimony and making it possible for God to use your family for His purposes. Something as simple as organization can open new doors of hospitality and ministry for you and your whole family. Don't squander those opportunities by disregarding something so easily remedied as a lack of planning and organization.

*H*

And when the wine gave out, the mother of Jesus said to Him, "They have no wine." And Jesus said to her, "Woman, what do I have to do with you? My hour has not yet come."

John 2:3-4

# Hovering Hinders

There's no doubt about it. We homeschoolers love our kids. In fact, we show that love everyday as we teach them, discipline them, encourage them, chauffer them, and the list goes on and on. The fact that we love our children so deeply is a wonderful thing; however, that deep and devoted love that we show them, unfortunately, often rears its ugly head in how we continually hover over them.

I'm not sure, but I'm afraid most, if not all, homeschoolers operate with somewhat of a chip on our shoulders. Oh, I don't think it's a chip that we've purposefully put in place, but it's there nonetheless. Whether it's because we've received negative comments from family and friends about our decision to homeschool or whether it's simply because we live in a culture that publicly denounces the decision of parents to educate their own children, we homeschoolers all seem to have something to prove. Because of this tendency in our hearts, it has been my observation after many years of homeschooling, that we tend to become hoverers.

What does it mean to hover over our children? The dictionary offers several definitions that seem applicable to us. First, to hover is to remain suspended over a place or object. Can you picture yourself? As your child is completing their math assignment are you leaning over their shoulder, quick to stop them mid-problem rather than allowing them to get it wrong? Why are we so afraid for our children to fail in their schoolwork? Is it because we've become too wrapped up in their academic success? If they don't score 100%, do we feel as though we've somehow failed? Homeschooling parent, we've got to get out of the way and allow our children to learn, succeed, and even fail without us jumping in to save them from those untimely failures. When they fail, it does not mean that we have failed them or that we are responsible for their failures.

Often, it is through our failures that we learn life's greatest lessons. Children who have become dependent on their parents to stop them before they get the answer wrong will never be able to incorporate those meaningful lessons that failure provides. They will lack the confidence to successfully complete their own work. They will quickly learn to hesitate rather than fail.... They will begin to hesitate just long enough for us to jump in and save the day.

I saw this hovering dynamic at work in my interactions with my youngest son. I may not have mentioned before just how much I detest teaching long division. Well, the process for my youngest son was no less painful than it had been for the older kids; however, Taylor hates to get anything wrong. He quickly realized that if he just stared at the long division problem long enough, I would jump in and walk him through the steps yet one more time. It didn't even bother him that I would become frustrated and short-tempered with him. At least, in his mind, he got the problem right without having to solve it and remember the steps all on his own. It took an older sibling pointing out what was happening for us to recognize and change his long division paradigm. Being forced to stay at the table to complete his long division regardless of what time it was, showed both of us that he actually was capable of doing the work himself. The loss of freedom he experienced when everyone else was done with their work and he was still harnessed to his, suddenly made it worthwhile to concentrate and answer the problems himself.

Academics are one thing, but the dictionary goes on further to define hovering as being in a state of uncertainty, irresolution, or suspense. Too many of us waste valuable time and energy hovering over our children's emotional and spiritual decisions. We try to baby-proof their worlds so that they won't be faced with temptation, they won't make bad decisions, and they definitely won't have to face the consequences of their decisions. This type of hovering will do nothing but handicap our children and produce spiritual hothouse Christians who are unable to function in a hostile world.

I'm like any other loving homeschooler. I wish with all my heart that I could keep my children from making bad decisions! However, I've seen the positive growth in their lives from some of what I would consider really lousy decision-making. It's absolutely our job to teach our children how to make good and godly decisions. It's certainly our job to fill their hearts and minds with the Word of God. It's unquestionably our job to stand firm and not waiver when it comes to accepting what is right and rejecting what is wrong, but, it is not our job, and we are totally inadequate, to coerce our children into always choosing wisely and into always walking faithfully with the Lord. When we hover and force spiritual decisions from young adults, we are simply teaching them to live like Pharisees, able to put on an outward appearance and conformity, with no real and vibrant spiritual life to sustain their actions. The Lord Jesus saved some of his sharpest criticism for this type of person. I certainly never want to encourage my children to adopt such a Pharisaical lifestyle!

Whether it's regarding academics, spiritual decisions, or relationships, our children definitely need our help, but they do not need us to hover over them worrying and fretting over the possibility of a wrong course of action. Sometimes, I think our hovering is less because of our love for our children and more because of our fear of embarrassment. We must never let our pride cause us to make poor parenting choices for our children. Yes, we should and must help them, but help does not mean coercion or forced decision-making.

The academic world has come up with a term to describe this type of parent. Deans of colleges across the country write and lecture about the detrimental effects of what they term "Helicopter" parents. They are recognizing the tendency of over-zealous and over-involved parents to want to micromanage the college experience for their children. They write of parents who argue with professors, demand special treatment, and generally continue the decision-making process for their now college-aged children.

Developmentally, these much-loved children are finding themselves at a disadvantage with their less parent-directed peers. Children who have grown up with hovering parents display troubling characteristics. First, they lack confidence. Because their parents have continually hovered over them by correcting their mistakes and assisting them with their work, they lack confidence in their own abilities. These are the students who are unable to meet deadlines and are caught by surprise that they can't have a "do-over" on their tests and papers. Growing up with hovering, performance-centered parents has built an unnatural dependence on reminders and second chances. Although sometimes it is appropriate to have your children re-take a test, make sure that it is the exception and not the norm. A poor grade on a paper or test may be just the kick in the pants they need to bump up their academic work ethic!

A second troubling characteristic of these students is their over-developed sense of self-importance. Because they were never allowed to fail and mommy or daddy has always swept in to save the day, these young people have grown up to believe that they and their needs are the most important priority for everyone they know. Inadvertently, their conscientious and hovering parents have taught them that they are the center of the universe. What a shock to be in the outside world and to suddenly be faced with the harsh realization that you are just a part of the crowd, no longer the center of importance. Please don't set your children up for this hurtful disappointment. Yes, our children are important, and dear, and precious to us, but they should never feel that they are the center of our universe and the utmost priority of our day. Teach them to work and serve as welcome members of your family unit. Allow them to make mistakes and be available to help them figure out how to resolve their difficulties, but DO NOT do it for them!

One final area of concern for these young adults shows up in their inability to build healthy relationships and make wise social choices. Because their parents planned their days, social activities, and even friendships, these young adults are somewhat handicapped when it comes to making those decisions for themselves. When our children are very young, it is possible and even easy for us to choose their friends and activities. However, as they mature and develop character, we should step out of the role of Activities Director and step into the role of Social Coach. I have always taken the time to get to know my children's friends. To be honest, some of their friends would not have been my first choice, but I believed that it was important for them to learn to make their own wise friendship decisions. I would ask them questions about their friends. Sometimes, based on their answers to me, I never had to say another word. They would realize the negative impact of that friendship and end it on their own. At other times I had to use my authority to ensure that time spent with friends I wasn't sure about was under our supervision; however, I still allowed my children to make those friendship decisions. We continually taught into what Scripture had to say about good and bad friendships. Believe me, there were some kids I just didn't like, but I attempted to minister to them in love. I prayed for them, fed them, and made myself available to talk and encourage them. Sometimes, all those troubled kids needed was an adult willing to invest in them and love on them.

By the time our kids are teenagers, they need to own the responsibility of their own friendship choices. Soon they'll be out of our homes and making those choices without our supervision. If they know that we are available as trusted counselors, they will feel free to seek us out. However, if their experience has shown them that we will tell them what to do and give them no rest until they comply, they will not come to us to seek wise counsel. Helping, not hovering, keeps the doors of communication wide open.

Obviously, it isn't just homeschoolers that deal with issues concerning hovering and over-controlling their children. The difference is this: As homeschoolers, we have exponentially so much more time to spend hovering. Don't do it! Take some time each day to manufacture some "purposeful neglect." Allow your children to fail. Force them to figure some things out on their own. Be available, but not indispensable. Finally, separate your children's failures and successes from your own pride. Allow them to grow, develop, and shine brightly as the Lord works individually and independently in their young hearts!

# Pray without ceasing.

I Thessalonians 5:17

# Infuse Your Homeschool With Prayer

Whether it is the initial decision to homeschool, what curriculum choices you will make, or how to handle a troubling relationship with a child, prayer should be our first line of defense. James 1:5 says, "If any of you lacks wisdom, let him ask of God, who gives to all generously and without reproach, and it will be given to him."

I can't begin to tell you how many times I have "lacked wisdom" when it came to homeschooling my children. I wish I could say that every time I lacked wisdom my first choice was to run to God in prayer. Sadly, too often I tried to come up with some sort of solution on my own, trusting that I didn't need God's help or direction. God is intimately aware of and concerned with your homeschooling decisions! He loves you and your children too much to see you wallowing in confusion or frustration.

When my oldest son began high school, I ran into my first major homeschooling brick wall. Up until that point I had chosen to have each of my children take responsibility for filling out their own daily work log. In the elementary grades and in middle school, this had been no problem. For some reason when this son reached high school, he just absolutely refused to keep up with that log. He faithfully did his schoolwork, but each day the log fell further and further behind. I became frustrated, then provoked, then full out angry. The logbook became a constant battleground between the two of us, and the tension spilled over to the rest of the household.

For months that logbook caused issues. The logbook became the focus of all of my training time with my son, and I couldn't recognize a single thing he did right. (And, there were lots of things he was doing right!) Looking back it's almost laughable how enormous that logbook became in my mind. I went to sleep thinking about the logbook. I woke up thinking about the logbook. The logbook loomed over my entire day. I fussed, I fumed, I cried, I threatened military school...but did I pray? NO!

Finally, after months of logbook turmoil in desperation, I took my problem to the Lord. As I sought His direction and His counsel regarding the situation, I began to realize that the logbook wasn't the real issue; it was just a symptom of a bigger issue between my son and me. By focusing on the logbook, I was totally missing the red flags my son was throwing up regarding another area in his life. When I was willing to make the logbook a non-issue and began to address the bigger issue instead, suddenly the logbook was filled in and all those battles were over. Guess I needed to take the "log"book out of my own eye! I wish I had gone to the Lord immediately with the issue, but the months of struggle taught me an important lesson: When I lack wisdom, God is eager to provide His wisdom!

All throughout the homeschool day you will be presented with opportunities to pray. Don't neglect those opportunities! When a child is struggling with their schoolwork and wants to give up... spend time praying. When a daughter is feeling unloved and unlovely, instead of a pep talk... spend time praying with her. When you feel ill-prepared to deal with a difficult situation during the day... spend time praying. Prayer is an open line of communication to God, and He is the one with the answers to our problems.

Sometimes, the answer to an off-kilter day is simply taking some time to pray with your children. It's okay to stop what you're doing and gather the troops for prayer. If one of your children seems to be having a particularly difficult day, taking them out of their normal routine and spending time in one-on-one prayer with them can be a soothing antidote to a rough day. With some of my children, taking a walk and spending time praying as we were walking helped that child to incorporate praying out loud into their life. The physical action of walking helped the mental juices of praying begin to flow.

Praying together to begin the homeschool day can set the tempo for a productive and peaceful day. Whether it's praying for one another or upholding friends and acquaintances in prayer, the discipline of starting our day talking to the Lord was a great reminder that He was present and involved in our homeschool.

Although it's important to pray throughout the homeschool year, I think two times of the year are of especial importance: before the beginning of the school year and at the end of the school year. Before the year begins, I would encourage you to pray about the routines, curriculum, and outside activities with which you will be involved. Without prayer it is tempting to over-schedule and over-commit our time and our children's time. Spend time praying over the year's calendar. It is much easier to say "no" to getting involved in a class or sport in the first place, than it is to attempt to gracefully back out once a commitment has been made. There are so many positive activities that our children can be involved in, but just because something is good doesn't necessarily mean it is the right activity for our children. Trust me, this is a lesson I learned from hard experience! We must not allow an overabundance of "good" things to rob us from experiencing whatever is the "best" thing for our home and homeschool.

When our children's schedules become over-crowded, they lose that valuable time they need to just be children. Our children need downtime to simply read, or daydream, or do NOTHING at all. Unscheduled, "boring" time provides our children the opportunity to be creative problem-solvers. Constant running from activity to activity is tiring to the whole family and can negate the good fruit we hoped to receive from the activity itself. I don't know about you, but when I am running around too much, my tongue gets a little sharper, and my patience gets a little shorter. Who am I kidding? When I'm running around too much my tongue gets much sharper, and my patience is totally non-existent! Prayer and careful evaluation can keep us from making hasty or unwise decisions about our level of involvement in activities outside of the home.

Another problem with over-scheduling our children is the fact that incorporating too many activities takes away from the important character training time that our children so desperately need. Good training, generally speaking, does not happen from the front seat of the car to the back. Repeated instructions and futile threats barked into the rear view mirror do nothing to change our children's hearts. When the majority of our time is spent driving to activities or trying to catch up on schoolwork when the activities are over, character training will be forced to take a backseat. Consider carefully and prayerfully what your homeschooling year will include and avoid becoming that parent who is continually beginning things, only to be forced to take them away later because of the bad fruit they are producing in your children's lives. This habit of continually giving and taking away will build bitterness and distrust in the heart of your child. Prayer and careful consideration on the front end of the school year will help us to avoid regretful decisions midway through the year.

Like the beginning of the school year, the end of the school year is another important time to bathe in prayer. Spend time at the end of the year asking the Lord to show you the positives and the negatives of the past year. Find a notebook and record what the Lord shows you through your time in prayer. Perhaps, He will bring to mind great areas of growth that occurred in your life or in your children's lives. Take the time to thank Him for that growth. As well, your prayer time may reveal areas of poor character that slipped by because of the busyness of the homeschool year. Record those areas and spend time throughout the summer seeking the Lord in prayer and developing a plan to deal with those areas adequately.

Praying without ceasing is a safeguard for our homeschools. Pray as you begin the year, pray throughout the year, and finally, pray as you end the year. Involve your children in those times of prayer and help them to see how personally involved God is with your family and your family's homeschooling decision.

*J*

**Whether then, you eat or drink
or whatever you do, do all
to the glory of God.**

I Corinthians 10:31

# Just the Means
# to an End

What goals do you have for your children and your homeschooling? If your end goal is simply a well-educated child who can find a great job, I hope you will reconsider that goal! I Corinthians 10:31 says, "Whether, then, you eat or drink or whatever you do, do all to the glory of God." God's goal for us and for our children is that we would become "God-Glorifiers." Therefore, the most important goal of our homeschooling should be to train up children who are equipped to bring glory to their God. With this goal in mind, academics and diligence in their studies will simply become a tool to assist us as we train our children to be God-Glorifiers.

It is so easy for academics to become the central goal of our homeschooling. Whether it is because our state requires completed workbooks or because we're afraid of what "They" might think, too often we neglect or ignore character development because the schoolwork just has to get done. It takes diligence and a commitment to character-healthy homeschooling to break the habit of an "academically-controlled" homeschool.

In order to keep academics in their proper place, we must be willing to stop what we are doing to deal with character issues. One of the beauties of homeschooling is the freedom we possess to focus on what is important at that very moment. Honest… trust me… the schoolwork will get done! However, if we disregard negative character issues in order to press on with school assignments, we are robbing our children of an important life lesson. The lesson is this: Developing and exhibiting good character is always more important that academic prowess. Exhibiting Christ-like character brings attention to our great God. Preening in our academic prowess only brings attention to us. Only one has any impact for eternity!

There were times in our homeschooling that I called a complete stop to the academics. These times were not a break or a vacation, but rather they were an opportunity to deal with negative character qualities I saw cropping up in our home and homeschooling. Sometimes, the negative character had to do with poor attitudes towards schoolwork. A week spent doing all of the dirty jobs around the house with little time off to do anything else, made my children thankful to return to their schoolwork the next week. Sometimes it was only one child who needed to be pulled out of academics. After dealing with the negative character issue, the extra time necessary in order to catch up on their missed schoolwork was an additional lesson and reminder to maintain their good character.

My second daughter, in particular, had a hard time maintaining a positive attitude about schoolwork. Because she is very bright, she felt that doing repetitive drills was simply beneath her dignity. In her mind, school was just robbing her of the much coveted freedom to get on with her life. I wanted her to understand how important an education was for her future, so I prayed about and devised a terribly repetitive and boring job to help her see that school was a blessing and that the "working" world wasn't as thrilling as she thought. Somewhere in one of our moves, we inherited a cheap and incredibly fake looking Ficus tree. Not something I would have ever purchased on my own, but once it found its way into our home the tree became a permanent resident. Since I can't keep houseplants alive to save my life, that cheesy Ficus tree was the only greenery in my home. Those trees have hundreds of little leaves, which had become hundreds of dusty little leaves. I handed Emma a wet wipe and told her to wipe each leaf, top and bottom. She wasn't allowed to do anything else until the Ficus was clean. That cleaning project took her several hours, and she was bored out of her mind. Afterwards, I talked to her about what types of jobs awaited an uneducated child: boring, repetitive, unrewarding jobs. Believe me, she was happy to get back to her schoolwork the next day! When her attitude began to dip, I had only to glance toward the Ficus, and she quickly pulled it together. She has her own home now with nary a Ficus in sight! However, what she does have is a great work ethic and a love for learning that just continues to grow.

It isn't just academics that can rob us of character-training opportunities. Any number of resume building activities can steal time from character development and spiritual training. Here in America success is defined by power, wealth, education, and position. So much of our day is spent preparing our children to become successful Americans. We want them to have the best education, be on the best teams, hang out with the best kids, join the most prestigious clubs, and get the best jobs. While none of these things are inherently wrong, when they become our primary focus to the neglect of character building, they become a wrong priority.

Jesus Christ was undeniably the most successful man who ever walked the earth. Two thousand plus years after His death millions still gather to worship Him and spread the good news about His life. However, unlike the American dream of power, wealth, prestige, and education, Christ's life was characterized by another set of descriptive words. Jesus Christ was reviled. He was spat upon. He was despised. He was poor. He was humble. He was a servant. He was meek. He was gentle. He was the companion of sinners. The list goes on and on.

How much time do we spend teaching our children to be successful in the way that Jesus was successful? Teaching them to be humble servants is the exact opposite of training them to be high-powered executives; yet, we say we want them to live like Christ. How can we reconcile these two vastly different worlds? As we make teaching healthy, Christ-like character to our children the primary goal of our homeschooling, I believe they will be successful not just as Christians, but in the secular world as well. Our world is aching for character-healthy, courageous leaders to stand up for what is right. When you make the conscious decision to subordinate all other teaching to the teaching of character, you are training the next generation of leaders; leaders that our world so desperately needs!

The lure of American success is strong. It is only through heartfelt conviction and steadfastness that we can keep what is truly primary the priority. Order your days in such a way that academics, sports, clubs, and jobs become teaching tools helping to train your children rather than masters seeking to claim your children.

**Consider it all joy,
my brethren, when you encounter
various trials, knowing that the testing
of your faith produces endurance.**

James 1:2-3

# Knotty Situations

It is an unavoidable fact that as a homeschooler you will encounter criticism, doubtful friends, and flat-out opposition to what you have chosen to do. It isn't so much what others say that matters; it is your response to their ill-timed and unwelcome words that will distinguish your family and the character of your homeschooling.

First, how can we deal with unwelcome criticism? Everyone has an opinion, and, strangely, when it comes to homeschooling, most people feel entirely justified in sharing those opinions. Not surprisingly, for most people their opinion of homeschooling is based on hearsay or just a strongly held belief that only "professionals" are adequate to teach our children. Often, my first response to these critical people is to defend my children and myself. I want to be just as vehement in my defense as they are in their opinion. May I encourage you that there is a better way to deal with critical people and their disparaging words?

In Proverbs 15:1 we are told, "A gentle answer turns away wrath. But a harsh word stirs up anger." When we make the conscious choice to respond gently and kindly to those who would criticize our choices, we are winning the right to share our hearts with them. An angry response simply verifies their faulty belief, but a gentle response will often open the door to further conversation. Many times as I have shared the benefits we enjoy as homeschoolers, our harshest critics have become our staunchest defenders. This includes my mother-in-law, who was vocally critical of our homeschool, my children, and our parenting in general. After a few years she began to tell other people that they should send their children to us to be homeschooled. What a radical change!

Your children's character-healthy behavior, exhibited during interactions with critical people, will often be your best defense. Even folks who disagreed with homeschooling in principle couldn't disregard the sweetness and others-oriented attitude of my children. Although there is a temptation to want to share homeschool statistics and success stories, resist the urge. Let the character of your family speak for you and watch as God begins to win over your critics.

What if, however, those same people remain steadfast in their disdain for homeschooling and in their attacks on your choices? Unfortunately, there have been times that we have had to stop spending time with certain friends because they felt the need to constantly tear down our homeschooling decision. We shared our convictions with them and asked them to respect those convictions, but at the point where they found that impossible to do, out of concern for our children, we had to distance ourselves.

If the aggressive critics are related to you, that becomes a more difficult situation, but again, I would encourage you to deal with those relatives in a humble and gentle manner. We can trust God to be our defender, and He will advocate for us. Remember, homeschooling is your family's decision and ultimately, it isn't anyone else's business how you decide to educate your children. I Thessalonians 4:11 reminds us to make it our ambition to lead a quiet life, mind our own business, and work with our hands. If we stay busy obeying the Lord in these areas, I believe that we can trust Him to protect and undergird our testimony.

To be honest, there have been times that even though I didn't want to hear what was being said; someone's criticism has been justified. We need to be willing to listen to what others say and to evaluate whether or not they have a valid point. If I am unable to accept any criticism, I am in effect saying that my homeschooling and my children are perfect. Far from it! James 4:6 says, "God is opposed to the proud, but gives grace to the humble." I want to have a humble heart when it comes to my homeschooling, and receiving criticism is part of God's humility program for me. Quite honestly, my daily failures as a homeschooling mother remind me of my imperfections, so when someone else points out a failure I'm not really shocked.

Just as a side note: It will always be easier to receive criticism, constructive or otherwise, about our children when we daily remind ourselves that those children are little sinners just like us. It is only when I begin to think too highly of my children that I catch myself shocked at what they've done. Let me share an example, although the child involved will go unnamed to protect their identity!

When I had five children whom I was homeschooling, I signed the children up for a homeschool swim class. Every Wednesday I would drop the children off at the pool and enjoy an hour and a half alone, well sort-of alone…just me and the baby. For those of you with many children, you know that being with just one child is sometimes just as good as solitude! One week I returned to the pool to find all of my children sitting outside on the bench, fully clothed and with dry hair. It seemed they hadn't been able to swim for long because someone had used the pool as a toilet. I loaded the disappointed children into the van, and we began the drive home. As we drove I talked to the children about how rude it was for someone to go potty in the pool. They all agreed, but as we talked I realized that one child was uncharacteristically quiet during the conversation. When we arrived at home I took that child aside and asked them the dreaded question: "Was it you?!?" They sheepishly looked at the ground and admitted that, yes, they hadn't wanted to get out of the pool, so they just…You get the picture.

Needless to say, I was horrified. At that moment I had an important character choice to make. No one knew who the "Potty Vandal" was and everything in me wanted to keep it that way! However, for that child's sake, it was important for me to crucify my pride, to help them face the consequences of their action, and to make restitution. I called the pool manager and explained the situation, telling him that I was bringing the culprit in to ask forgiveness and to see what they could do to help to fix the situation. I asked the pool manager not to be too easy on my child. You know how it is… people feel sorry for children and tell them that their offense was no big deal. In this case, I absolutely wanted my offspring to know that this was a HUGE deal, so that they would never do it again!

I shouldn't have worried about the pool manager being too lax. Oh no! He came out with verbal guns blaring and told my child just how rude and inconsiderate their action had been. He went on explain in great detail the work and cost involved in emptying, scrubbing, and sanitizing the pool. In the end he accepted my child's apology, but he made it clear just how disappointed in them he was and how he expected better from them in the future. Trust me, I didn't need to remind my child not to repeat their crime; they didn't ever want to go through a talk like that again! Don't let pride keep you from recognizing your children's capacity to do, say, and participate in shocking activities. Take a deep breath, pray for wisdom, and face the unpleasantness head-on. Those situations provide great lessons for not only our children but for us as well.

Criticism and opposition will come. As we deal with those issues in a gentle and Christ-like manner, we will be showing our children by example what it means to be kind, patient, long-suffering, and forgiving. Don't miss the opportunity to teach these important character qualities. Your testimony of good character and patience with those who don't understand your family choice will affect your children more than someone else's criticism ever could!

For He says, Order on order,
Line on line, Line on line,
A little here, a little there.

Isaiah 28:10

# Learning To Love The Basics

Just as important for me as learning to slow down, learning to prayerfully make our homeschooling decisions, and learning how to deal with criticism has been, homeschooling for twenty years has taught me the importance of learning to love the basics. The basics are called the basics for a very obvious reason: They are the basis of all that my children need to learn. By the very nature of their name, the basics are not very exciting. Skills like reading, the multiplication tables, penmanship (Yes, I still teach penmanship.), and good citizenship aren't the subjects that make my children's hearts race and entice them to rush to the schoolroom in eager anticipation; however, these are the very subjects that form the stepping-stones necessary for everything else they want to learn.

Taking time to master the basics teaches our children some very important character qualities. It takes perseverance and diligence to memorize the times tables, and while it's being done it isn't immediately obvious how helpful this basic skill will be in the years to come. It takes humility and submission to erase a line of crookedly scrawled cursive letters and to rewrite them, numerous times if necessary. It takes patience to learn all of the phonetic sounds and to slow down and take the time to sound out words when you just want to know how the story ends. Learning good citizenship and manners requires embracing the character qualities of respect and deference for others. No, the basics aren't very exciting, but without them our children would be lacking major lessons of basic character.

One simple word comes to mind when I think about teaching the basics. That word is repetition. Galatians 6:9 says, "Let us not lose heart in doing good, for in due time we will reap if we do not become weary." In the same way that repeating the basics over and over until they have mastered them teaches our children important character qualities for life, steadfastly working with our children as they struggle to incorporate those basics will build strong character in our lives as well.

As I shared before, teaching long division (a basic) has been the most consistent and repeated training ground for patience building in my life. Not a single one of my eight children found long division an easy subject to learn. In fact, I think more tears were shed over long division than over any other subject we studied and that includes my tears as well! When I began the process one more time with Taylor, my youngest child, I thought for sure that I was going to lose my mind! God reminded me again not to grow weary in well doing, and that my example of patience and perseverance would help Taylor to patiently persevere as well. Finally, he has mastered the steps of long division, and I am looking forward to my retirement as a "Long Division Instructor." I'm trying to convince God that I've learned my lesson about patience, so that my own kids don't ask me to help teach long division to the grandchildren!

May I share with you, from painful experience, that skimping on the basics will come back to hurt you later. Do whatever it takes to make sure your children master the basic knowledge they need to open the doors to further learning. Use flashcards, memory games, technological helpers, whatever is necessary to complete the task at hand. Don't assume that the passage of time will teach the lessons they need to learn.

I have always believed that spelling is as much about genetics as it is about academics. I have a strongly developed photographic memory so spelling has never been an issue for me. I simply close my eyes and picture a word, and then I am able to spell it accurately. Three of my daughters are very much like me when it comes to learning. They have strong photographic memories as well, and they just naturally spell words correctly. Because spelling is so easy for me, I just couldn't understand how my other children could struggle so much with their spelling words. I thought they were just being lazy or inattentive. I wrongly assumed that everyone "saw" the words in their heads like I did, and so I didn't spend the time necessary to teach them the basic spelling rules they needed to succeed in spelling. What a mistake! A couple of my older children still struggle with their spelling, and it has made life in the professional realm much more difficult for them. Don't assume your kids will just "get it" later. Spend time while they are young insisting that they work hard and master the basics. Even when it seems like a child has mastered a basic subject, periodically go back and review what they have learned. The extra review will help to cement the lessons in their minds and will maximize retention of that basic skill.

Honestly, mastering the basics probably won't earn our kids any kudos from the grandparents or neighbors, but regardless, the basics are a necessary part of life. As our children are faithful to learn these unexciting subjects, they are building strong character muscle which will help them as they work through other more exciting, and often-times more difficult, subjects. Make sure that you are diligent in prais-ing them for their hard work in the tedious and mundane subjects. Praise them for their perseverance, their diligence, their patience, and their faithfulness. Don't simply praise them for the finished product, but praise them for the character they exhibited in the process of learning. Tell them how proud you are of the strong character they are building through their hard work in learning their foundational subjects. When we praise good character in our kids, we are encour-aging them (literally infusing them with courage) to want to build and incorporate even more good character into their lives. The basics will become attractive when they see that not growing weary in well doing has brought about God-honoring character growth that is rec-ognized and admired by you, their parents.

Allow me to say it one more time… Don't neglect the basics! Today, you won't win any Parent of the Year awards from your kids as you consistently insist on repetition and mastery of the "boring" subjects. However, someday they will thank you for your diligent encouragement of their efforts. Maybe they'll even ask you to teach their kids, the ultimate homeschooler compliment!

*If the whole body were an eye, where would the hearing be? If the whole were hearing, where would the sense of smell be?*

I Corinthians 12:17

# Make The Most Of Learning Styles

Notice I did not say, "Be a slave to learning styles." Learning styles, or more simply, the way our children best assimilate information, is an important part of home-schooling, but learning styles are simply a tool to be used to our benefit.

Many, many books have been written about the array of learning styles that different people employ. Some go into lengthy and detailed descriptions of how brains function and how to tailor a different educational system for each learner. I'm just not that complicated. Or, maybe my brain's just not that big! For me, with eight learners in my home, I see three primary learning styles. The Listener, The Looker, and The Toucher. Although there is some overlap among these learning types, all of my children have been predominantly one of the three types.

The Listener is a learner that assimilates information best through hearing or listening. My son, Nate, is a Listener. He can listen to an audio book and relay, in great detail, everything that he learned. From a very young age, when he heard jokes he would have an uncanny and often unstoppable ability to repeat the jokes. Unfortunately, discovering what was and wasn't appropriate took a little longer for him to learn! Because most educational curriculum is not designed for listeners, Nate had a rough start to his academic adventure. Learning to read was a difficult task for Nate because learning to read necessitates looking at letters and remembering their sounds. Because he learned primarily by listening, just seeing a letter written on a page didn't jog his memory. To him each day seemed like he was learning new letters instead of a review of what he had learned the previous day. For him, it took extra tutoring and a commitment to mastery to get beyond an Easy-Reader level.

For a child who is a Listening Learner, there are just some subjects that must be learned in a learning style that is not their strength. It isn't possible to learn to read simply by listening. It isn't possible to learn to write simply by listening. I had to encourage Nate that although some subjects were harder for him as a listener, he still needed to have the commitment to learn those more difficult subjects. Commitment is an important character quality, and often it is learned through adverse situations. For Nate, reading was that adverse situation. Thankfully, he persevered through the difficult lessons, and today he is a prolific reader, often staying up late at night to finish whatever book has currently captured his heart.

The majority of my children are Looking Learners. They learn best when they can read a lesson or look at an instruction book. For Nate, I could simply tell him a list of chores I wanted him to complete, and he could complete the chores with no difficulty. For my other children to be successful, I needed to write down the list and put it in their hands. Not everything in life is written down, so for my Looking Learners I have spent time teaching them to listen carefully.

With these children I will verbally give them a list of instructions for a lesson. Then, once I have given the instructions, I will have them repeat those instructions back to me, word for word. If they get it right, great! If not, we start over and repeat the exercise until they can echo back what I have told them. Even though it is easier for them to read and learn, they need to be able to learn by listening as well. A good exercise for these kids has been learning to take sermon notes. Without the self-discipline of writing down what they are hearing, many important lessons would simply go in one ear and out the other.

My husband is a strong Listening Learner, and I am an equally strong Looking Learner. Working together in ministry has forced us to learn how to merge our learning styles. When Steve was completing his doctorate, he would ask me to critique parts of his thesis. When he read the thesis aloud to me, he would hear the parts that didn't flow or needed to be changed, even though I didn't hear it; however, when I would sit down and read what he had written, I could find errors or areas that needed some fine-tuning. In the same way, when I am writing I look at what I've written, and because it is grammatically correct, it seems fine. Steve, on the other hand, listens to what I've read and helps me to make the flow of my writing more natural. We're a good team that way!

Because I so strongly learn by looking, it is sometimes tempting to plan my children's school days and curriculum around "looking" types of activities. What a bad idea! I have to continually remind myself to adapt and bend with the other learning styles present in our home. Just teaching my children to learn in the same way that I learn would handicap them from growth in areas that aren't "looking" related. Consider how you are teaching your children. If all your teaching is safely within your own learning style, it's time to step out of your comfort zone and adjust your teaching to encompass other types of learning. Good news! In the process you will be stretching yourself and making learning in new and different ways a normal pattern for your own life.

My youngest child, Taylor, is a Toucher. He learns best when he can physically manipulate a subject. For him, math would be impossible without manipulatives. He learned his letters by using magnetic alphabet tiles on the refrigerator. He is extremely skilled with Legos and K'nex. However, like the other two categories, not everything can be learned via touch. To help Taylor develop the other learning styles, I have set aside time each day for him to read silently and also to spend time listening to story CDs. As I have him narrate back what he has read or heard to me, he is developing good Listener and Looker habits.

Knowing our children's learning styles is a helpful tool in homeschooling. We can, as appropriate, provide ways for them to learn within their learning styles. However, learning styles should never become a crutch or an excuse for our children. We live in a diverse world, and they must discipline themselves to learn in diverse ways. The character qualities of diligence and perseverance will help them become well-balanced learners. We, as their parents, must find ways to stretch them and to help them begin to feel comfortable learning through all three means: Listening, Looking, and Touching.

The beginning of wisdom is:
Acquire wisdom;
And with all your acquiring,
get understanding.

Proverbs 4:7

# No Curriculum Does It All

When I was twenty years old and met a new person, their first question to me was always, "What college do you attend?" My husband is an airline pilot, and when he meets new folks within minutes they will ask him, "What airplane do you fly?" Different ages and professions are defined by different questions, and it is no different with homeschoolers. Soon after meeting another homeschooler, the question invariably is asked, "So, what curriculum do you use?" Our curriculum choices, or lack thereof, seem to be the defining standard for homeschoolers.

The amount of curriculum offerings to choose from is overwhelming! Curriculum fairs around the country draw large crowds and provide myriad choices when it comes to educating our children. So, what makes a certain curriculum the right choice for our family? Although I can't give you a definitive answer to that question, allow me to share some observations about what I have learned regarding curriculum over the years.

First, with rare exceptions, I believe that a consistent and involved parent could produce excellent results with almost any curriculum. It isn't the curriculum that teaches our children; we do! Even if you are using a video curriculum, it is your involvement and interaction with your child that is going to make that video curriculum a viable alternative or a disappointing waste of money.

If you asked me what curriculum we use, my answer would change depending on what year of homeschooling you asked the question. Different seasons in the life of our family have necessitated making different curriculum choices. In the same way, different families have different homeschool structures to their days. While some families are most comfortable with workbooks and fill in the blank questions, other families will crave read-aloud and narrative studies. Neither choice is right or wrong. They are just that - choices.

For most of us the problem comes when we take a perfectly good curriculum that is having wonderful results in someone else's family, and we assume that it will automatically have the same great results for our family. Choice of curriculum, like homeschool style, needs to be a prayerful family decision. Once you have prayerfully made your decision, you will have the confidence necessary to forge ahead with your curriculum choices, regardless of what everyone else is doing.

When I am introduced to a new curriculum, I try to take time to evaluate that curriculum and to consider how implementing it would work in my home and with our unique children. As a new homeschooler, too often I got caught in the trap of adding a new curriculum to what we were already doing just because I heard it was beneficial or just because everyone else was using it. When we change direction in our homeschools continually in that way, we are behaving like a bunch of sheep that just follow the crowd, chasing the newest, greatest thing, and simply doing what everyone else is doing. Don't be a sheep parent. Be brave, and follow God's leading for your own special family!

Do you think peer pressure is only at work in young people's lives? Many new homeschoolers absolutely feel pressured to do whatever the rest of their homeschool friends are doing. While sometimes this may work out, other times it simply puts added pressure on the early years of homeschooling. Yes, we should take advice and consider what other people are using to teach their children, but ultimately we must make appropriate family decisions. Curriculum should never become a divisive issue with parents judging one another's choices; instead, we should become helpful resources to encourage one another.

Having said all that let me share some of the curriculum choices we have made over the years. Remember, I'm not encouraging you to blindly follow what the Scheibners did, but I'm hopefully offering you tools to assist you in making wise decisions for your family.

When I finally realized that my expectations for learning were WAY too high for our first year of homeschooling, I prayerfully chose a complete curriculum by one publisher. Since I was just getting into the swing of homeschooling, I felt that using a comprehensive curriculum would keep us on track and would give me the time I needed to build my homeschooling muscles. That curriculum worked well, kept me organized, and provided me a jumping off point to branch out the next year. Even today, I still use some resources from that same publisher, but I don't use a complete curriculum from any one source.

Since that first year, I haven't felt the need to use a comprehensive curriculum. Instead, I spend time throughout the year researching products, asking questions, and evaluating how a certain curriculum will meet the educational needs of each child. I don't necessarily use the same curriculum with each child; instead, I evaluate their learning styles, interests, strengths, and weaknesses to help me make wise decisions.

With any curriculum my children use, mastery and retention is my goal. Therefore, I look for curriculums that incorporate built-in review. I like textbooks that build upon a foundation of knowledge, rather than working as a compilation of standalone lessons. Whether it's reading, mathematics, history, or science, retaining what they have already learned has been the key to my children mastering a subject.

For math, especially in the elementary grades, I would encourage you to pick one curriculum for each individual child and stick with it. Jumping back and forth between math curriculums has the tendency to produce gaps in your child's learning, which are difficult to overcome and only make your job harder. I look for math texts that are not too "busy" on each page. Too many cartoon drawings or an overabundance of problems on one page has always been a distraction for my children. Honestly, it isn't the amount of problems they complete, but the quality of the problems offered that will help our children to successfully master the basics of mathematics. Remembering the chapter on learning styles, if you have children who love to learn math with manipulatives, great! However, if your children have no need for those manipulatives, don't force them to use something that doesn't help. The goal is that they are learning their math concepts, not necessarily becoming master flashcard and decimal rod manipulators.

In my mind, learning to read is the most important and necessary foundational skill my children must master. If they can read, and read well, they will always be able to research and learn whatever they need to know. Find a curriculum that you are comfortable with and just dive in. Unlike math, if a curriculum just wasn't working, and I didn't see my child progressing at a consistent rate, I was willing to try something new. Although most of my children used Teach Your Child to Read in 100 Easy Lessons, for one child that just wasn't adequate, and we had to branch out.

Take the time to teach phonics! Some children just take off reading, and it doesn't seem necessary to do phonics review.... Do it anyway! Their competent grasp of phonetic rules will prove invaluable as they learn to spell increasingly more difficult words. For our family Explode the Code made phonics fun and easy and provided an effortless segue to spelling lessons. After Explode the Code we transitioned to SRA language studies, and for all my kids that curriculum built a firm foundation in reading and grammar.

There are so many wonderful grade-level reading series. I tried to choose reading books that told great stories. I wanted my children to be drawn into their books and captivated by the characters, not preached at. (They have me for that!) I really liked using series that told continuing stories of familiar characters. One example of this type of curriculum would be the Pathway Readers. These readers told stories of different families and the activities and adventures these families embarked upon. As my children worked their way through this series, they built relationships with the characters and looked forward each day to reading more about their escapades. Another great series is the Christian Light Press readers. These books follow the same format as the Pathway Readers, sharing stories of courage, ingenuity, history, and many biographical stories. Unlike the Pathway books, this series is full color and beautifully illustrated. Beyond their reading books, as soon as my children could read alone, I assigned a certain number of books that had to be completed during the school year. I assigned which books they needed to read, but they had the freedom to choose in what order to complete the books.

Some of the early reader series that my children enjoyed included: Hank the Cowdog, The Bobbsey Twins, Amelia Bedelia, Henry and Mudge, and Encyclopedia Brown. As their reading skills increased, I added series such as: Nancy Drew (the older books), The Hardy Boys, All-Of-A-Kind-Family, and The American Girl History Mysteries series. My older children dove into Elsie Dinsmore, G.A. Henty, and individual books written by distinguished authors.

For my older students, I loved the Learning Language Arts Through Literature Gold and Silver textbooks. By high school I didn't feel like the kids needed to be focusing as intently on grammar any longer, so instead we focused on literature and interacting with literature through writing. Regardless of what curriculum you choose, make sure your high school students are writing, writing, and writing. Having the skills necessary to communicate well via the written word will open many doors of opportunity for our children. For many years, each morning I would hand my children a short writing prompt, for example: "This morning I looked under my bed and…." I would then have them write a one-page story built around the introductory sentence. All of my kids became very comfortable and confident in their writing skills and in their ability to imaginatively create a well-written story.

Although I used various textbooks and resources as tools, I never purchased a complete history curriculum. My children learned history through biographies, non-fiction books, and historical fiction. They ALL love history, and each child has developed their own area of expertise. Even my youngest, Taylor, who is only ten years old, has a specialty. Ever since he was five years old, he has been fascinated with the sinking of the Titanic. As each year passes, his storehouse of knowledge about that historical event grows and continues to develop. As a springboard to learning for my elementary school children, I enjoyed incorporating lessons from The History of the World by Susan Wise Bauer.

When it comes to choosing a science curriculum, be careful what is being taught. There is nothing neutral when it comes to science curriculums, so for our family it was imperative to choose a curriculum that taught science from a Creationist perspective. There are many great curriculums to choose from, but my children especially liked, and more importantly understood, the teaching of the Apologia curriculum. Sometimes I think that I learned as much as they did while we studied Biology, Chemistry, and Physical Science. Just a helpful hint…Make sure that your children perform their biology labs outside or in a well-ventilated room. I learned from sad experience just how long it takes to get that awful formaldehyde smell out of the house! Trust me, you don't want to go there….

My younger children worked their way through one or more of the Christian Liberty Nature Readers each year. As they read these incredibly detailed books, it became habit to notice the wildlife around us and to begin to keep nature journals and photo diaries.

One year we deviated from the norm and spent the entire year using Unit Studies by Amanda Bennett. Although we continued with our regular math curriculum, everything else we studied came from the unit studies. What a wonderful year of learning as my children delved deeply into a wide variety of topics. They studied Government and Politics, the Pilgrims, Airplanes and Flight, Sea Life, Photography, and much more. For one son, learning history, math, and geography was made more interesting by studying those subjects in the context of a Baseball unit study. In hindsight, I wish I had known about the Amanda Bennett studies for young children when my kids were all smaller. Her neat "Lap Books" make learning fun and exciting for early learners!

What about handwriting? I have always really enjoyed the Reason for Writing curriculum. The constant repetition of basic skills has seemed to give my kids a good foundation in legible handwriting. Although I know that cursive has fallen out of favor in many schools, I still require my children to learn this skill. Even though we, as a society, have begun to use computers and electronics to communicate, my children still have dear elderly friends who write them sweet notes in cursive. Without learning how to read and write in the cursive style, our children will lose the ability to understand the communications with this older generation. As well, our country's most important documents were written in the old and beautiful style of cursive writing, and I want my children to be able to read and appreciate those original documents without having to re-write them in manuscript or see them on a computer screen. As an added bonus, learning cursive will help to develop some wonderful character qualities in our children's lives. Think about it, patiently learning to form cursive letters teaches our children persistence, due diligence, carefulness, and submissiveness.

Spend some time thinking about the areas of learning that are more difficult for you to teach. Don't be afraid to get help in those areas! Art and music are the two areas that come to mind for me. Although I tried some "Just add water" types of do-it-yourself curriculums, ultimately, it made more sense for me to find help to teach my kids in these areas. Bartering with a friend, or in some cases hiring a tutor or teacher can take the stress out of teaching that more challenging material.

In choosing curriculum remember...more isn't necessarily better. Using what you have, consistently and diligently, can produce just as impressive results as having bookshelves overflowing with textbooks and resources. Also, don't forget the valuable resources that are available at your local library. Although the Internet is a wonderful tool for research, it is important that your children know how to easily access what they need from the library. Take the time to get to know your librarians. To a person, they have always been delighted to help us find what we were looking for, and often, they pointed us to resources that I didn't even know existed.

Whatever curriculum you use, unless it is teaching unBiblical facts or causing your children to regress rather than progress, I would encourage you to stick with it for the entire school year. Changing programs in mid-year is difficult for our kids and doesn't teach them the self-discipline of working through a less than perfect situation. Committing to sticking with a curriculum even when it's not exactly what we expected, will keep us from unnecessarily wasting money and building bad habits of giving up too easily.

Curriculum choices don't need to be overwhelming or frightening. Thanks to an amazingly vast array of choices, we have the opportunity to research and discover what works best in each of our own unique family situations. Then, well prepared, we can confidently make whatever curriculum we choose work productively for us and for our family.

# Beloved, if God so loved us, we also ought to love one another.

I John 4:11

# Observing Relationships

If there is one area where homeschoolers should excel, it is in the area of family relationships. Sadly, however, some home-schoolers spend every day together, but whether because of busyness or a lack of intimate involvement with one another, family relationships are lacking or in some cases non-existent. As Christians, this should never be the case, and homeschooling provides a great avenue to avoid distance and cultivate intimacy among family members.

Proverbs 27:23 admonishes us: "Know well the condition of your flocks, and pay attention to your herds." Homeschoolers, this is our charge from God concerning our children. Our children are our assigned flock, and we are to pay attention to what is going on in their lives. This verse doesn't tell us to worry about the neighbor's flock, or our sister's flock, or even the pastor's flock. We are to know well the condition of OUR OWN flock. Regardless of what it takes, eliminate any distractions from your life that keep you from studying and evaluating the state of your little God-given flock.

Simply spending time together every day will not guarantee that we know the condition of our flock, although such a large quantity of time is helpful. To really know our flock, we must study them intently. We must pray for keen ears and eyes to see and recognize what is truly happening behind the scenes in our homes. Just because everything seems calm on the surface, we must practice diligence to ensure that what is happening in public is an accurate representation of what is going on in our children's lives and hearts.

Remember, your children are not simply a group that all thinks, acts, and responds in unison. Each of your children is a God-formed individual, and in order to cultivate a relationship with each individual child we must be attentive to who they are and what is happening in their independent lives and hearts. Each individual child will need us to reach out, respond, and react in uniquely loving ways in order to truly know them and to build deep heart-bound relationships with them.

How can we cultivate relationships with our children? Well, when I want to cultivate a relationship with a friend, I spend time with that person. I find out what is important to my friend. I seek to listen to their heart when they speak not just to their words. I find ways to be a blessing to them. I pray for them and serve them as often I can. When necessary, out of love for my friend, I confront error in their life. However, because I care about the relationship, I do any such confrontation in love and with the goal of restoring my friend to a right relationship with God.

So it is to cultivate a relationship with our children. We must get to know them. We must get to know what excites them, what frightens them, what overwhelms them, what thrills them. We must learn their little quirks. We must learn ways to show love to them, and perhaps even more importantly, we must affirm that we like them and that we would choose them to be our friends even if they weren't our children.

Rather than viewing our children as a group, we must commit to taking time to be alone with each child and to spend time participating in things that each special child enjoys. As we are transparent about our hopes, dreams, fears, and wishes, our children will learn to be transparent with us, as well, and our relationships will grow and flourish. Time alone doesn't have to be lengthy, but it must be frequent. The anticipation of a special time with mom or dad will thrill our children's hearts, so we must be careful to fulfill our promises when it comes to making that special time happen.

Homeschooling provides a wonderful opportunity to cultivate deep and abiding relationships between siblings also. Sibling rivalry is NOT an important developmental step, nor is it the natural outcome of having more than one child. Yes, with more children there will always be conflict, but with more children comes more opportunities to teach our children how to resolve conflict in a Christ-like manner. As our children learn to work through their conflicts, seek forgiveness, and restore relationships with one another, they will begin to build deep and thoughtful interaction with one another. No, it doesn't happen overnight, but it is well worth the effort involved in teaching them these important and Biblical conflict-resolution skills. As they learn to resolve conflict, they will be learning important character qualities such as: love, patience, humility, compassion, long-suffering, and more. Take advantage of every opportunity that sibling strife brings your way to teach these essential virtues.

In our home, Peter and Emma had the hardest time learning to co-exist and care for each other. With only 18 months between their births, the two seemed to compete against each other from the time they were toddlers. We never allowed them to fight or hold grudges against one another, but instead, we insisted that they communicate clearly until any conflict was resolved. At one point, they found themselves sharing chores, free time, and their own dinner table, as we pushed them to build a friendship with one another.

Fast-forward 18 years. Today, Peter and Emma have graduated from the same college, which they attended together for three years. Both have married, and they live within fifteen minutes of one another. They, along their spouses, spend every holiday together and often get together midweek to play board games and eat dinner. Soon, Peter and his wife will be relocating to North Carolina, and Emma is mourning the loss of her brother already. She and Peter shop together, goof off together, and spend time praying for their other siblings together. Looking on over the years I sometimes doubted that they would ever get past simply tolerating one another. God has done a tremendous work in their hearts and in their friendship. In fact, the final chapter of this book is an afterword written by Peter and Emma together.

Side note: Since I first wrote this chapter, Peter and his sweet wife, Rochelle, did relocate to North Carolina. This past fall, they delivered their first daughter as a stillborn baby. As we all gathered for the funeral, it was Emma who brought the most simple and quiet comfort to Peter's grieving heart. She arrived ready to serve, and she prepared meals and cooked for the gathered family, giving us time to take care of other important details. She spent so much time simply standing next to Peter with her arm around his waist, and I saw him gain strength and peace through that special relationship with his little sister. God has indeed given them something special, and they treasure their relationship fiercely.

Don't give up the fight when it comes to cultivating close relationships in your family. From the beginning, remind your children that God chose each member of your family, and He knew that your family was the perfect mix of personalities from His point of view. We always reminded our children that they needed to work hard to be good friends because one day we would be gone, but they would still have each other. Although some relationships in the family are naturally closer than others, I know my children love each other, and that they will always go to bat for each other. Around our house it's definitely, "I can tease you, but nobody else better say anything mean about you!"

There will be times as you cultivate your family relationships that one member of the family may need more attention than the others. Don't hesitate to extend the extra time that is needed. Teaching the other children that life operates on an "as-needed" basis rather than a "fairness" basis is an important lesson. Just because one family member is in need of extra time or compassion doesn't mean that we have to balance the scale with every other child. As they learn to sacrifice their time with you, out of love and concern for their brother or sister, they will be learning compassion and the importance of others. Don't rob them of this character lesson by trying to make sure that your time is always divided evenly.

Sometimes it seems like God has especially equipped mothers to be the relationship cultivators in the home. Because we spend such large amounts of time with the children, we often notice discouragement or changes in behavior more quickly than dads can. Mom, don't keep this information to yourself. Share what you are seeing with your husband and together minister to the needy child. Work as a team to discern the needs in your family and to build strong family relationships. For single parents, God is your ally. Seek His face when you are in doubt about what is going on in a child's life and include God in the conversation with your child. It brings security into a child's life to know that God is intimately involved and concerned about every area of their life. My single-parent friends have shared with me that they gain courage and security as they are reminded of God's intimate involvement in their parenting challenges.

God put your family together carefully and on purpose. He wants us to take advantage of every opportunity to build and cultivate the relationships within our families. Homeschooling is a wonderful tool to fulfill that calling and build those solid family ties. Grammar and math lessons may soon be forgotten, but close family relationships will last for a lifetime. Take the time to build those relationships and enjoy the fruit of your labor.

Be anxious for nothing, but in everything by prayer and supplication with thanksgiving let your requests be made known to God. And the peace of God, which surpasses all comprehension, shall guard your hearts and your minds in Christ Jesus.

Philippians 4:6-7

# Practicing God's Peace

When I talk with other homeschoolers, I hear a predictably common refrain. Homeschool moms, and I would assume non-homeschooling mothers as well, all struggle with worries and concerns about our children. Because we love them so deeply, it is almost impossible to eradicate all of our concerns. We worry about their education. We worry about college. We worry about their future. We worry about their spouses-to-be. We worry about their health, their spiritual life, and the list goes on and on.

It seems so simplistic to say that the solution to our problem is to entrust our children to God, but that truly is the answer. The God of the universe is intimately concerned about our children. I know this is hard to believe, but He loves them even more than we do! How we deal with our concerns has the potential to either influence our children to grow closer to the Lord or to learn to mistrust Him. Either they'll grow in courage as they see us handing our fears to God, or they'll shrivel in worry as they witness our example of doubt and fear.

We can't simply make our worries go away, but we can take pro-active steps to actively hand our worries over to God. For me, the greatest antidote for my fears regarding the children has been the memorized Word of God. Verses like I Peter 5:7, "Casting all your anxiety on Him because He cares for you," and Philippians 4:6, which reminds me to: "Be anxious for nothing." are a safeguard for my heart. May I encourage you to search your Bible for verses that will help you to hand your cares over to the Lord, and then to commit those verses to your memory? When you wake up at night with your heart racing in fear, those hidden verses can calm and quiet your soul.

It has been so helpful to me when I remember that only God knows the end of the story with each of my children. There have been times with each child that I found myself disappointed or discouraged. I wondered how they could make the choices they were making and struggled to see how any good could come from their decisions. Remembering that I only see the here and now while God knows how He will use those struggles in their lives has helped me to continue to entrust my children to Him.

When Emma was 18, I had a friend design a bracelet for her. The bracelet had an engraving that said, "My good; His glory." For months, we had been reminding Emma that everything that came into her life had been approved by God, even the hard things. We discussed that God's responsibility was to use those events to bring about good in her life. (Romans 8:28) Emma's job was to ensure that she was bringing God glory throughout the process. (I Corinthians 10:31) Emma wears the bracelet, but the lesson contained on the bracelet is an equally important lesson for me as well. The situations that seem so impossible or unworkable in my mind are designed to grow and mature my children. I can't cause that growth or maturity (although I sure wish I could), but God can cause exactly the growth and maturity He desires to see in my children's lives.

We live in a scary world, and our children face very real dangers; dangers, which are not only physical but also spiritual and emotional as well. Worrying about these unknown dangers can deposit us firmly in the "What-if" zone. Although God has promised to give us the grace to deal with whatever comes into our lives, He has never promised to give us the grace to deal with the what-ifs of life. His grace is sufficient for all of our needs; grace for something that isn't even real would be nothing more than wasted grace. I have to be honest here, if every bad thing I worried about actually happened to my children, none of them would still be around today! Instead, God instructs us to take our thoughts captive and to focus on Him, and Him alone. (II Corinthians 10:5)

This area of entrusting our children to God should be one of our greatest ministries to one another. As we spend time with our homeschooling friends, we have wonderful opportunities to re-mind one another of the faithfulness of God and of His constant watch care over our children. I'm afraid that too often our times together become task-oriented and wrapped up in conversations about curriculum and extra-curricular activities. How often do we walk away from those times just wishing that someone knew the cares and concerns that were threatening our hearts. I'm sure that if I feel that way there are many other moms dealing with the same heart fears. May I encourage you to be the first kid on your block to share your heart with others who can then provide you with the prayer and encouragement you so desperately need. Sometimes, all it takes is one person willing to be vulnerable, in order for others to feel safe sharing their own fears. We should be one another's best cheerleaders and safe havens. Sure, curriculum and extra-curricular activities are important, but don't miss the opportunity to strengthen, encourage, and undergird one another in this exciting, yet at times, fearful, adventure of parenting and homeschooling our precious children.

I wish that I could give each of you a hug and tell you that it's all going to be okay, but I can't. All we as parents can do is faithfully, consistently, and obediently follow God's direction as we teach and train our children. The rest is up to Him. We can entrust our children to God because we know that He is faithful, and that He watches over our children better than we ever could! Share the good news of God's faithfulness with someone who needs that encouragement today, and you'll be encouraged to remember this simple truth as well.

# 2

Blessed is the man who perseveres under trial; for once he has been approved, he will receive the crown of life, which the Lord has promised to those who love Him.

James 1:12

# Quashing Curve Balls

Have you ever had "one of those days?" You know the type of day I'm talking about...the one where everything just seems to go wrong. Often, and somewhat predictably, those days come when I am the least prepared to deal with them. It is when I'm sure that I have it all together, my plan firmly in place, that the out of whack days seem to appear.

My off-kilter days often begin like this....The night before I will fill out the next day's to-do list. I lay out the children's clothes. I make sure the chores of the day are completed and the meal plan is in place for breakfast. I get to bed at a decent hour congratulating myself on what a good job I have done preparing for tomorrow.

When the alarm clock goes off, instead of hitting snooze I get up and spend time with my Bible and the Lord. Now, I know it will be a good day because God owes me, right? Wrong!

That morning, without a doubt, something will go wrong. Whether it's a sick child, an unplanned and unpleasant phone call, cross words with my husband, or a myriad of other plan killers, something will happen to disrupt my carefully laid plans. I call those plan killers "curve balls" and I have realized over these past twenty years of homeschooling that God orchestrates the curve balls in my life to remind me that I am not in charge; He is.

Curve balls do not bring out the best in my character. Curve balls are the events that cause me to grumble, complain, and sometimes throw an all-out pity party. Still, God continues to throw me curve balls. Why? I've finally realized that God throws me curve balls because He loves me, and because He wants me to learn to "quash" those curve balls to His honor and glory. (Isn't quash a great word? I just love it!)

Here's the untarnished truth. On the days that everything goes my way and my plan runs smoothly without a hitch, I'm a pretty nice person. I exhibit character qualities like peace, patience, kindness, gentleness, love, and self-control on those days. Those are the days that, although I wouldn't verbalize it, I begin to live like I believe that I'm a pretty exemplary Christian. Isn't it just too bad that more moms can't be like ME! My Pharisaical pride takes over, and I hurt myself by trying to pat my own back.

That's when God throws me a curve ball, and again, He throws me that curve ball because He loves me. God throws you curve balls because He loves you, too. He knows that I am pretty good at hitting fast balls (those days that go my way), but He also knows that when I'm squeezed by a curve ball what is truly on the inside oozes out. God loves me too much to see me hold onto that yucky, character-less garbage that pops out when I get thrown a curve ball. So, with that growth in mind, He continues to throw me curve balls over and over so that I will learn how to hit them accurately.

This entire fall was a perfect example of God's curve ball training in action. For the first time in years, I actually had all of my lesson plans laid out for ALL of the children and for the ENTIRE year! Oh yeah, I was feeling pretty good about myself! The previous several years of traveling with my husband to speak at parenting conferences had made it clear to me just how important it was to have the kid's schoolwork prepared well ahead of time in order to facilitate their studies while I was gone on the road. This year, I had it all under control. As usual, our first couple of weeks of homeschooling went very smoothly. Those filled out planners were working great; however, my reverie wouldn't last much longer.

In early October, a series of incidents made it crystal clear that it was God's will for our family to relocate. Suddenly, I was flying to North Carolina to house hunt. After finding a suitable house, I came home to face a three-week deadline to pack and relocate our family. For Steve, those three weeks were a busy time of speaking and airline trips. Needless to say, my perfectly planned school year hit a major bump in the road, and we've been recovering ever since. What a curve ball! Thankfully, the literally hundreds of curve balls I've faced in the past ten years had been preparing me for such a moment, and, hopefully, God was glorified as we pressed on to the new plan.

I'm not there yet, but I'm learning. Now when a sick child disrupts my oh-so-important schedule, instead of responding poorly I'm learning to respond mercifully. When a cross conversation leaves me feeling sorry for myself, instead of stewing all day I'm learning to humble myself and seek forgiveness for my part of the conflict. One swing after another I'm learning to hit those curve balls.

Homeschooling isn't just about our children growing and learning. Homeschooling is as much for us as it is for them. A family of sinners spending inordinate amounts of time together is fertile ground for conviction and growth. Sometimes we strike out when God throws us a curve ball, but the more often we practice swinging the easier the curve balls will become and the more often we'll succeed at meeting our goal: bringing glory to our God in the midst of the curve ball.

Our children get thrown curve balls as well. Often their curve balls show up in disappointment over quashed plans or in the conflict of an unresolved issue with a friend. We must teach our children to hit curve balls as well. Sometimes, as their mom, I just want to comfort my children and allow them to feel sorry for themselves. Although it is important to comfort them and sympathize with their pain, it is equally important to teach them how to exhibit good character even in the midst of disappointment and hurt. As we teach them pro-active problem-solving skills and guide them to seek forgiveness and restoration, we will be going far in preparing them to successfully quash the curve balls they are thrown.

Curve balls are an inevitable part of life. We can get angry when they come, or we can learn to be thankful for the curve balls of life. Don't try to avoid them or duck away from them. Face curve balls head on and learn to hit them out of the park with a mighty character-weighted swing!

Come to Me, all who are weary and heavy-laden, and I will give you rest.

Matthew 11:28

# Rest, Reading, and Other Routine-Breakers

Although I would be the first person to encourage you to have an organized plan and routine for your homeschooling, I also believe that there are days we should just take off! One of the greatest freedoms that homeschooling has afforded my family is the freedom to take a day and spend it doing something completely off the schedule.

Have you ever taken a day and just read aloud through an entire book? My children love when I read to them. They are always disappointed when we end a chapter, and they must wait until the following evening to find out what happens next. Sometimes, not all the time, but sometimes, I will call a day off from our regular routine and spend the day on the couch reading the entire book to them. We pop popcorn, make hot chocolate, and we read and read and read. Those days are so sweet for me as our children take turns sitting beside me and snuggling on the couch. Now that I have older children, they often take turns reading to give my voice a break. In fact, my daughter Katie is such an eloquent reader that we beg her to read aloud on our family road trips. On one such trip, she read the entire unabridged version of The Princess Bride. If you loved the movie, let me assure you that the book is even funnier and extremely well written!

Taking the day off from school may seem simply like a vacation day, but I believe it can be so much more. Great literature teaches our children important character lessons. As they listen to their favorite characters moving through the story and making decisions, both good and bad, our children will begin to associate with those characters. Often, talking about a character's choices opens doors for communication that might otherwise be nailed shut.

I absolutely cannot stand the cloying books that hit my kids over the head with one character quality or another. When a title tells us that the book is about sharing, or lying, or cheating, or pride, I feel like the book is insulting to my children's intelligence and discernment. Great literature doesn't broadcast its moral message; instead, it respectfully allows the readers to discern the moral message on their own. When my kids discover the truth of a moral lesson on their own, they are much more willing to incorporate that lesson in their own lives. Take advantage of great literature. In the resource section of this book, I have included an abbreviated list of wonderful books that will captivate and involve your children. Again, your local librarians can be a wealth of information to assist you in finding suitable books. As a warning, if you haven't heard of the recommended book, and especially if it is a recent copyright, take some time to preview and look through the book to be sure that it aligns with your family's personal convictions.

Another time to take a day away from the regular routine is to have a creativity day. Sometimes schoolwork can become nothing more than another workbook page completed or another test taken. Take time off from the normal school day to plan a day of creative ideas. Whether it's building a western fort out of sticks or baking a special recipe from a time in history that we've been studying, these creative days not only build great memories, but they also help my children put some of their head learning into action.

For some children, there is another hidden but important benefit to these not-so-normal school days. A few of my children have a tendency to get married to the schedule. They are only comfortable if everything goes exactly as it has always gone, and the predictability of their day is not disrupted. While those predictable days may be more comfortable for them, that is just not the way life works. One of the only things we can count on is change, and our rigid and routine children need to learn how to go with the flow without falling apart. Flexibility is an important character quality, and these children will not learn flexibility if they can insist that their days always follow the same predictable pattern. Mix things up for them, and teach into the out of control feelings they experience. Remind them that things will return to normal soon, but that everyone needs to learn to flex and cooperate with a change in plans. With my organized personality, it's important for me to change the routine sometimes just so I don't bore my kids to death!

Sometimes, our children just need to break the routine in order to have some downtime. There are seasons of our ministry that require a great deal of hands-on work from our entire family. Our children spend hours binding books, filling boxes, and collating papers. This type of indoor busy work is oftentimes exhausting for them. After a stretch of busy ministry days, they may need to just go outside and have the freedom to run, dig, climb, and explore without feeling as though they are being negligent with their schoolwork. Other children, although they hate to admit it, just need to sleep for a while after working for us. When I give them the freedom to lie on their beds and read, they often fall asleep for many hours and wake up refreshed and ready to get on with life. Such breaks in the routine are more than acceptable; they are necessary to the functioning of our family.

For the most part, our homeschool days do follow a very predictable routine. We make sure to complete the necessary subjects, and we follow the lesson planner closely. However, taking days off to do special projects and to spend special time traveling through a book have provided our family with great memories and special mementos.

Don't allow the clock or the calendar to rule your homeschool. Take advantage of the freedoms that homeschooling brings to your family. Take the day off and spend it building those special memories. The workbooks will get done and your children will complete their educations and head off on their own. Special times with your family can't wait forever; take advantage of every opportunity while your family is still all together!

**Do nothing from selfishness or empty conceit, but with humility of mind let each of you regard one another as more important than himself.**

Philippians 2:3

# Stop the Competition

I'm pretty sure that I was born competitive. In the same way that I didn't have to teach my children how to lie or how to say no, no one had to teach me to be competitive; I just was. When it was dinnertime, I raced to be the first one done. When we got into the car, I raced to be buckled first. When I went to little girl birthday parties, I took the games seriously and always tried to win. It didn't even matter that no one was competing against me; I still looked at everything as a competition.

This is a true, take-it-to-the-bank statement: Homeschooling is NOT a competitive sport! Sadly, however, many homeschoolers treat homeschooling as though it is a competitive sport. This spirit of competitiveness can only cause discord within the homeschooling community, and it adds to the negative stigma that society attaches to homeschooling families. Do not allow yourself to join the ranks of competitive homeschoolers!

What does competitive homeschooling look like? Perhaps it is because I have spent my entire Christian life trying to unlearn my competitive tendencies that competitive homeschoolers stick out like a sore thumb to me. Their competitiveness shows up in two ways: What they say, and what they do.

You can recognize a competitive homeschooler by their spirit of one-upmanship. Regardless of what you or your children are doing, they have done something better. Regardless of what curriculum you choose, they have a better curriculum. Instead of congratulating or encouraging the achievements of others, they change the subject to extol their child's achievements. Now, I believe that we in the homeschooling community should be one another's greatest cheerleaders. I love when folks share their triumphs and successes with me, and I appreciate the freedom to share my children's exciting achievements with other homeschoolers. This is not the type of communication that a competitive homeschooler can enjoy.

I truly believe that much of their competitive communication comes from a real lack of confidence. Because they are not comfortable and confident in their own homeschooling, they feel the need to make sure that their listeners realize just what a good job of homeschooling they are doing. I feel sorry for many of these parents, and wish I could just tell them to relax and enjoy homeschooling without feeling the need to compete.

How can we avoid becoming competitive in our communication? It is quite easy. When everyone else is talking about the great things that their children have done, resist the urge to jump in and share our children's accomplishments as well. Certainly, there are times that we, in a spirit of humility, will share our children's successes. However, while there are plenty of talkers in this world, there is a great lack of listeners. What a wonderful opportunity to simply listen, congratulate, and encourage another homeschooling parent or child. Sometimes, my children will ask me why I didn't share their achievements when everyone else was sharing success stories. I remind them that it doesn't always have to be about us. There is a great blessing in just rejoicing for others and being happy for someone else's success.

If you are uncertain whether or not you have stepped over the line in your communication and become a competitive homeschooler, might I encourage you to limit the amount of successes you share with others? Work hard to become a compassionate listener. We all need someone to share our exciting news with, so pick a faithful friend or family member who will be excited for your children without feeling threatened by your communication. Use them as a sounding board to discuss your children, but with others become the friend who can be counted on to listen and encourage.

Interestingly, more and more homeschoolers are responding competitively regarding negative areas in their children's lives as well as in sharing positive successes. If you attend many homeschool meetings, you will often notice a downward spiral of parents sharing escalating horror stories about their children's poor behavior with the parent of the worst child coming out as the seeming victor. How shameful! Years ago parents didn't share their children's disobedience in a proud way. Instead, they were embarrassed by poor character and dealt with those issues in private. Don't allow yourself to be drawn into those types of conversations. You will damage your children's testimonies and be tempted to exaggerate their shortcomings in order to fit in with the other parents. Personally, I would encourage you to walk away from any conversation that focuses on poor behavior in a way that glorifies a lack of character.

Homeschool competitiveness shows up in the activities we allow our children to participate in as well. More and more, I am meeting parents that are proud to tell me that their children graduated at sixteen, or their children were babysitting at eleven, or their children worked full time at a very young age. While some of these activities might be acceptable for some children, I'm afraid that our competitive culture is encouraging parents to rush their children into inappropriate responsibilities. When we engage our children in activities or responsibilities that they aren't old enough or mature enough to handle, all we do is puff up our own pride and encourage our children to think more highly of themselves than they ought to think. We can't allow pride to drive the decisions we make for our children. If an activity or responsibility seems questionable for your child, slow down and take the time necessary to prayerfully consider whether or not it is an acceptable choice and one that will lead to a wise outcome.

Unfortunately, too often our competitiveness has breached the walls of the homeschooling community and seeped into our relationships with others who make different educational choices for their children. I'm not sure how the "Mommy Wars" began, but they do nothing to further the Kingdom of God. Although we should be fully convinced of our family's decision to homeschool, our family's decision has no right to infringe on the choices of another family. God calls different families to different choices, and I don't believe that being a homeschooler makes us any better than any other family!

Families, whether homeschooling or not, need all of the encouragement that they can glean from one another. Our society is doing all that it can to tear down the family and competitive homeschoolers don't need to add to that destructive dynamic. It is simply pride and arrogance that causes us to think we have the answer to every family's educational decision. Instead of judging one another, we must find ways to encourage and uphold one another. It is so sad to see church fellowships divided into homeschooling and non-homeschooling groups. All parents love their children and want what is best for them. Let's pray for one another and for our children and trust God to clearly and specifically direct each family as He sees best.

Within our own home, sometimes we use competition to spur one another on to better accomplish our goals. However, outside our four walls, competitiveness will do nothing to further relationships with others. In fact, it will cause discord and distance in relationships. Do your best, do what's best for your family, and be happy for the successes and accomplishments of others. Be careful not to get trapped in the throes of competitive homeschooling.

And be kind to one another, tender-
hearted, forgiving each other, just as
God in Christ also has forgiven you.

Ephesians 4:32

# Teaching into "Duh", Dawdling, and Other Delays

Some days my kids just don't get it! Whether it's blank stares when I ask them a question or painful dawdling over their seatwork, there are days that school just isn't happening. How can we handle those days in a constructive rather than destructive way? In other words, how do we keep from destroying those annoying children?! Children, who, by the way, God chose specifically to bless our family with and to build our character, too.

Our first line of defense is to diagnose the source of the "duh" or dawdling problem. Even though I hate to admit it, there are days that for one reason or another, my children just physically aren't up to doing their schoolwork. Whether it's mental, emotional, or physical sickness, they just aren't up to the task at hand.

I'm one of those moms that just automatically assume that my children are well until they absolutely prove otherwise. When Emma was 18 months old, I slipped coming down the stairs while carrying her. Of course I would never drop my precious little girl, so I held onto her tightly as we bumped, bumped, bumped all the way down the stairs. Unfortunately, as all that bumping was going on, Emma's chubby little leg was between my rear end and the stairs. She cried quite a bit initially, but soon she seemed fine. Except for one little problem…she just wouldn't put her foot down.

I assumed she was just sore and laid her down for a nap. There was no way I thought she had broken her leg. All through that nap my mommy intuition was in overdrive, but I just couldn't believe she had a broken leg…. No way! Boy was I wrong! When she still wouldn't put her foot down hours later, I took her to the Emergency Room where they discovered she had broken her leg...in two places. "Horrible Mommy" moment! For the next six weeks, my adorable and VERY verbal 18 month old told everyone who would listen, "Mommy broke my leg in two places!"

After Emma's accident I found myself taking my children's complaints about aches, pains, and sore throats more seriously. Yes, sometimes they just don't feel up to their work. Sometimes I don't feel up to my work! On those days, I need to extend mercy and sympathy. I don't need to "Bring the hammer down!"

Other times the choices that their father and I have made lead to an off-school day. When the Red Sox were in the playoffs and made it to the World Series, I allowed my children to stay up for all of the games. Needless to say, they were all dragging every day and our schoolwork suffered. I felt like it was a priority decision, though, because who knew when the Red Sox would make it that far again…. A very real concern for anyone in Red Sox Nation! I treated their duhs and dawdlings the same way then that I treated them when the children were sick.

There are times, however, my children are giving me blank stares or dawdling over their schoolwork for no good reason. At those times, it is my responsibility to make sure they get to their work and stick at it until they have done it and have done it completely. I hate feeling like a taskmaster, but it is important for our children to learn how to do what needs to be done, even when they aren't in the mood.

We have tried to teach our children this important lesson: 90% of life consists of doing things you don't want to do in order to get to the 10% that you love to do. In other words, "You don't have to like it; you just have to do it." That simple truth has been an important lesson for me as well. I love cuddling with my babies and reading them books. I don't love changing diapers and cleaning up vomit. Both come with the territory when it comes to having children. The sooner our children learn to complete the unpleasant tasks first in order to get on to the fun stuff, the better off they will be in life.

Some children are absolutely characterized by dawdling. It is the overwhelming habit of their life. When you have been fighting the battle over and over it becomes tempting to try to excuse their dawdling away. Resist the urge! Do not allow them to rationalize their dawdling, and certainly don't hand them a ready-made excuse. When our children hear us telling other people that it just takes them a little longer than everyone else to get their work done, we have just handed them an excuse. Instead, we need to help our children be successful in putting off their dawdling habit and in putting on diligence at doing their work in a timely manner. For the consistent dawdlers in your home, a timer is a wise investment. Decide what a reasonable amount of time for an assignment should be, add five minutes, and let the timer run. Ahead of time, lay out consequences for not meeting the time requirement and be consistent in enforcing those requirements. Come on! You know your children can move quickly when they want to, just offer an ice cream cone at the end of their assignment and see how quickly they'll plow through that work. Don't be afraid to teach the important character lessons of timeliness and appropriateness, even when it means facing a battleground.

Sometimes, it is tempting to just call it a day; the battle doesn't seem worth the effort. May I encourage you to stick it out and insist on your children finishing their work? In our ministry we have had the opportunity to spend time with several college deans and professors. To a person, these men and women have been impressed with the maturity and responsibility shown by the homeschooled students on their campus; however, every single one of the campus leaders we spoke with also mentioned the same problem with their homeschoolers. The students who had been educated at home had a problem sticking with their work and meeting deadlines. For many of these students, college was the first time that they had been given a deadline that actually meant anything.

Those college students didn't all develop that same habit completely on their own. We, their parents, assisted them in developing those sloppy completion attitudes. Every time they had a lazy or blank-stare school day and we gave up trying and just let them quit for the day, we were training them that assigned work could be put off until they were in the mood to get it done. Sorry, but real life doesn't work that way. As conscientious homeschoolers, we need to ensure that our children know how to stick with a job or an assignment until it is done and done right.

With my youngest two students, Stephen and Taylor, I've realized that sometimes they give me a "duh" answer in hopes that by stalling they will get me to provide the answer for them. Be careful not to be trapped by this manipulation! If you find yourself "help-ing" continually with basic skills or repeating directions over and over, stop and insist that your children listen carefully and complete the work on their own. Interestingly, one year I homeschooled a young man whose parents had sensed he was failing in a class-room setting and sent him to me to be homeschooled. Every time I asked him a question, he looked left and right waiting for someone else to answer. Bad news for him…he was the only one who could answer my questions! Another example, one of my own children would ask me questions when he was taking a test. I had to remind him that none of his public school friends had the luxury of asking the teacher to "fill in the blanks," and I wasn't going to grant him that privilege either. Our job is to teach our children how to learn not to do the learning for them.

Sometimes, even if they are not actually dawdling, it becomes obvious that our children are just going through the motions, do-ing their work to get the check in the block. Just getting it done has never been my goal for our homeschooling. I continually remind the children that God doesn't want them to simply be willing learn-ers. In learning their school subjects, just as in every other area of life, God wants them to be eager participants in their own growth. Don't accept a habitual attitude of willingness; instead, teach into the valuable character quality of eagerness. Evaluate your children and your school routine and pray about what needs to change to ignite their hearts to eagerness. Eager hearts bring glory to God. School work is really just the training ground for real life, and I am convinced that if my children learn to approach whatever needs to get done with an eager, rather than simply a willing heart, they will be noticed for their great attitudes and win the opportunity to share that their attitude comes from a commitment to glorifying their great God.

Duh and dawdling days will come. They're not the end of the world! However, make sure that there is a legitimate reason for the delay in schoolwork, and if there isn't, insist on an excellent finisher's attitude. Your training now will prepare your children for leadership and quality workmanship in their future endeavors.

*U*

**But one and the same Spirit works all these things, distributing to each one individually just as He wills.**

I Corinthians 12:11

# Unique Talents and Strengths

With eight children in our homeschool, we have quite a variety of special talents and areas of strength and giftedness. It is our privilege, as our children's teachers, to encourage and build up those differing gifts. It is an unfortunate child who is expected to be a cookie cutter replica of all the other children in the family.

How do we evaluate our children's areas of strengths and giftedness? Not to be overly simplistic, but often we can see our children's strengths as we observe the activities that delight their hearts and bring them excitement. My husband calls it, "Seeing what rocks their boats." We must be careful to wisely evaluate those areas, and we must make sure that we aren't trying to see something that doesn't exist just because we hope a child will go in a certain direction.

119

Once we've discovered our child's unique talents or interests, what a joy it is to provide resources to help them develop in that area. The opportunities for homeschoolers are endless, and the flexible hours of homeschooling make it possible for our children to be involved in many unique activities while other children are still attending school. Let me share some of the ways that my children's very different personalities developed into unique and special talents and strengths.

My firstborn, Katie, was always a musical child. From the time she was little she hummed and sang through her day. As with all of our children, when she began school we began piano lessons. Katie did well at the piano, but I wasn't really noticing anything special. One Sunday she came home from church and announced that she was trying out for the lead in the church Christmas musical. Although I knew she loved to sing, I didn't really think she had much of a chance of being chosen for the lead. The next Sunday she won the coveted lead, and the director came to talk to us about her beautiful singing voice. Honestly, I had focused so much on piano that I didn't really pay attention to her singing. Katie did a beautiful job in the lead role, and we began to invest in voice lessons for her. Today, Katie still uses her voice to sing special music at her church, and she leads the children's choir and teaches piano. Music is her strength and passion.

Peter is our second child. From an early age Peter loved to run things and to set up elaborate games and plays. When he was a young teenager, we gave him an inexpensive video camera, and he began to make films. At first the films all had a common theme: A giant (Dad) was taken down by a determined, albeit small knight (Taylor). Soon, however, Peter began to gather the other teenage boys and make longer and more elaborate films. At one point, he made a short documentary about a highly decorated Vietnam veteran in our congregation. When Peter was 16, he assisted a director from Los Angeles in filming our ministry's Parenting Matters DVDs. With the knowledge he gained from that experience, he and his friends then filmed, edited, and produced our Character Matters series. With each project he was honing his skills and building a resume. Peter entered college as a filmmaking major. In August of 2011, he released his senior project titled, In My Seat, to YouTube. This 15-minute documentary chronicling his father's 9/11 experience went viral and has been seen in nearly every country around the world. Today, Peter is on staff with a large church where he is their Director of Audio, Video, and Lights. He is already making plans for his next short film. He lives out his passion and his strengths every day.

Emma has always been the child that is the most like me. She and I spent hours together in the kitchen, and from an early age she loved to cook and invent recipes. When she was a teenager, I assigned her the job of planning, purchasing, and preparing the family meal once a week. Remember we're a family of 10, so that was no small task. She loved the challenge! Emma entered college as a Culinary Art/Business major. She graduated #1 in her class and is working her way up the chef ranks. Providing Emma with the tools and the freedom to explore her love of cooking has led to a career that she has embraced wholeheartedly.

Molly's strengths lie in her ability to make people feel loved and accepted. For a while, I tried to push her to learn cello. She enjoyed listening to cello music, so I assumed she would like to play the cello as well. Besides, I thought she looked like a cello player! Sometimes "interest in" doesn't translate into "passion for." Because of Molly's desire to interact with and help other people, when she was 16 she confided in us that she wanted to go to South Africa to help missionary friends of ours begin a new work with high school girls. I understood her desire, but she was only 16. I was hesitant to allow her the freedom to pursue her dream; however, we had always tried to encourage our children's passions, so with fear and trepidation we allowed her to plan her trip. She traveled alone to South Africa and had a wonderful time building relationships on that trip that continue today. Molly is a social butterfly, and she uses her people skills to draw people out and make everyone feel welcome in her little world.

Nate's talents lie in designing and visualizing projects. When he was very young, we tried to capitalize on that by providing him with high quality building sets. His other passion is history, and he spends hours reading G.A. Henty books and discussing battle strategies with me. His father and I wondered what direction Nate would choose to go once he graduated from high school. After much prayer he has decided to study Residential Construction while earning his Bachelors of Applied Science. We can see how that major will encourage his designing and building skills. Nate is also thinking about joining the military after he graduates from college, incorporating his love for strategy and battle plans. Some of his interests that I wrongly assumed would just pass away as he got older have instead grown stronger and stronger.

Unlike our older children, our youngest three children are athletes. Sometimes the older children complain that they didn't get to be on sports teams, but not a single one of them ever showed any consistency in any athletic endeavor. For Baleigh, Stephen, and Tate, even if they weren't on an organized team, they would still be passionately practicing their chosen sports. Baleigh lives in the water. She participates on two swim teams and works as a lifeguard at the YMCA. She was chosen to be co-captain of the public high school swim team even though she is a homeschooler. Baleigh sleeps, eats, and dreams about swimming. She hopes to earn a swimming scholarship to college and continue competing.

For Stephen and Taylor life is all about baseball. They participate in winter sports only because they want to stay in shape for baseball season. For both boys, the dream is to become a professional baseball player and to eventually play for the Boston Red Sox. I must admit that I would be thrilled with that dream coming true! Who knows what will become of their dream? But for now, our job is to provide them with opportunities to hone their skills and build their reputations as good team members.

Neither Steve nor I are professional athletes. Neither Steve nor I are musicians. Neither Steve nor I are particularly gifted at design. Yes, we have shown interest in many of those areas, but they are definitely not our passions. Our children don't need to mimic our passions, and we don't necessarily have to be passionate about what thrills them. To help them be successful, we just need to be excited for them as they explore what causes them joy and excitement. This entails being good listeners and a wise sounding board for their dreams and desires. We don't need to make their dreams happen for them, but we certainly don't need to be dream killers either. We just need to free them to pursue their God-given talents without the fear that somehow they are disappointing us.

I hope this brief snapshot of our children's strengths and talents gives you an idea of the diversity you might find in your own family. If we had tried to make them all musicians, or all athletes, or all filmmakers, we would have squandered the individual talent that God placed inside of each of them. Our job isn't to tell them what to become but to help them discover what they are passionate about.

Just a side note: Until children are older, late teens to early twenties, their passions may change often. Don't lock yourself, or them, into a specific dream while they are still young. Instead, offer them broad opportunities to grow and develop in many areas. For example, for years our daughter Baleigh played the violin, switching to fiddle five years ago. She loves the fiddle and at one point dreamed of majoring in violin/fiddle in college. That dream has changed now, but she still plays the fiddle and finds great joy in sharing her music with others. It would have been easy to be disappointed when she changed direction, but we really do want her to follow the passions that God has placed in her heart.

When it comes to our children's special talents and strengths, we must again become students of their lives. As we pray with them and for them, and as we provide resources and opportunities for them to pursue their interests, we will begin to see their unique gifts emerge. What a privilege God has given us to shepherd our children as they grow into the special young people He has designed them to become!

# V

### And let us not lose heart in doing good, for in due time we shall reap if we do not grow weary.

Galatians 6:9

# Valium Isn't the Answer

Before I had children dinnertime and the hours right after dinner were my favorite time of the day. With work done for the day, I could snuggle with my sweetie and catch up on the day's events. Then came babies. Suddenly dinner became the arsenic hour with everyone hungry and me tired. After dinner was bath time and stories to end an already exhausting day. In fact, I remember once when Steve was gone on a Navy deployment, I put all four children in the bathtub and then realized that I just didn't have the strength to get them out again. I have vivid memories of sitting on the toilet lid, looking at my bubbly children, and wondering what would happen if I just drained the water and covered them with blankets. Thus goes the thinking of a sleep-deprived mommy.

No! Dinner and bedtime are no longer my favorite time of the day. They've been replaced by "The Looking Hour." The Looking Hour is that time of the day when I can sneak into my children's bedrooms and just gaze at their beautiful sleeping faces. Watching them, so sweet and lovable in their jammies, is usually all the fuel I need to get me psyched up to face another tiring day of diapers, meals, lessons, discipline, laundry, and more. That Looking Hour brings closure to one day and allows me to begin the next with a fresh and hopeful attitude.

As my children have gotten older, however, sometimes the difficulties of one day threaten to spill over into the next day. While homeschooling affords us wonderful time together, it also means that we have more time than the average family to offend, injure, or damage one another. Thankfully, God has provided us with a process to deal with those grievances and to begin each day with a fresh start. That process is the process of forgiveness.

I don't know why asking forgiveness seems to be such a difficult thing for us to do. Although my children will say, "I'm sorry," teaching them the Biblical standard of seeking forgiveness is a continual process. We all want to allow the passage of time to take the place of seeking forgiveness. It is true in my own life, and I see it in my children's lives. We hope the ticking of the clock or a good night's sleep will take care of the relationship problems we are facing. Sometimes, I just try to shrug it off, proclaiming the offense "no big deal." A close look at the second half of Ephesians 4:26 has caused me to rethink this attitude.

In Ephesians 4 Paul exhorts his readers to "Not let the sun go down on your anger." For a long time, I assumed that the anger Paul was referring to was a big blow-up or absolute rage. A closer look at the original language revealed a convicting truth. The word used for anger in this verse is a Greek word that is translated "mild irritation." In other words God's standard for me was to end the day with even the mildest irritation dealt with in a Biblical manner. This certainly changed my "no big deal" perspective, and learning to extend and receive forgiveness became an essential priority and a central part of our home and homeschooling.

For us, the first step in learning to ask forgiveness was realizing our need to be forgiven. When we don't ask forgiveness, it is like having a wound that we don't clean out. If we just stick a band aid on a dirty oozing wound, pretty soon infection sets in and the wound begins to fester and stink. When we allow conflict to go unresolved, pretty soon the whole family is affected by the infected stink coming from our relational wounds. Admitting wrongdoing is the only way to begin the process of cleaning out a wound, and forgiveness then becomes the antibiotic that facilitates healing.

Asking forgiveness is different than apologizing. Today, in polite society, we apologize. We say the words, "I'm sorry," and the offended person politely responds, "That's alright, no big deal." Whether that is how they truly feel or not is a different story. Saying I'm sorry may tell someone how we feel about a problem, but it doesn't take ownership of our wrongdoing, and it doesn't give the other person any chance to restore with us.

Instead of apologizing, our whole family began to practice asking forgiveness of one another. When we taught the children how to ask forgiveness, we instructed them to say the words, "Will you forgive me?" and then to insert the wrong attitude, action, or character quality they had displayed. For example, "Will you forgive me for taking your toy? That was selfish of me." As the children were forced to think through the specific nature of their wrongdoing, they understood more clearly how they had caused offense. On the other side of the relationship, as the offended person was offered the chance to extend forgiveness, they could be sure that their brother or sister really understood what they had done wrong. Asking forgiveness, instead of simply apologizing, keeps our children from a hastily muttered, "I'm sorry," words which are usually just intended to end the problem and cut the conversation short not to resolve the real issue.

Moms and dads, it is just as important for you to keep a short list of offenses with one another by seeking forgiveness appropriately. Your example of humility as you deal with one another and the inevitable daily offenses will speak volumes to your children. Growing up in a home where mommy and daddy ask each other for forgiveness will provide security for your children. It really is true; our children can face anything when they are confident that their parents truly love one another. When we, as the adults in the home, allow bitterness and anger to fester, we make everyone walk on eggshells. There is no security, and our children will struggle to complete the simplest of tasks because they are worried in their hearts about your relationship. Even if it means delaying dinner or taking a break from your teaching to make a phone call, be quick to make amends and to restore in a way that is obvious to your children and a blessing to one another.

Asking forgiveness and offering forgiveness appropriately helps our entire family keep a short list of offenses. Sometimes one or both parties need a little time to think about what went on, but we try very hard to deal with offenses quickly and completely. When each day ends with peace within the family, it makes it possible for the next day to start new and fresh.

I must be honest here. Sometimes it seems easier for my children to forgive me and one another, and then move on from the incident. I am working hard to learn how to practice the practical side of forgiveness, which means allowing the forgiven one to move on and restore their relationship with me. When I don't allow them to move on, we can't start fresh and I bring old problems into our new day.

If you still have little children, enjoy The Looking Hour. The days pass so quickly and soon those little children will be tucking you into bed. (Don't laugh. I'm usually in bed long before my teenagers these days!) Make forgiveness the daily practice in your household and enjoy the freshness of each new day…a new day with no mistakes in it … yet!

Now for this very reason also, applying all diligence, in your faith supply moral excellence, and in your moral excellence, knowledge; and in your knowledge, self-control, and in your self-control, perseverance, and in your perseverance, godliness; and in your godliness, brotherly kindness, and in your brotherly kindness, love.

I Peter 1:5-7

# We All Learn Together

Besides homeschooling, what activities are you passionate about pursuing? What are you spending time researching and studying for your own personal growth? Once I made the decision to homeschool, I quickly found myself spending all of my free time immersed in the homeschooling culture. I read about homeschooling. I researched curriculum. I spent time on Internet homeschooling boards. My life became nothing but homeschooling, homeschooling, and more homeschooling. As all of our conversations became consumed by the children and homeschooling, my husband gently pointed out to me that I was losing who I was and becoming nothing more than a child-centered homeschooler. It was time for some self-evaluation.

As I prayed about my priorities and the time I was investing in homeschooling, I came to some realizations about myself. The first was this: When people asked me about my life, I defined myself as a homeschooler. Homeschooling had become my identity, and I knew that such a narrow delineation was not my goal.

First and foremost, I am a follower of Jesus Christ! I am not a homeschooler who is a Christian; rather, I am a Christian homeschooler. When homeschooling becomes my identity, I lose my ability to witness for Christ, and instead find all of my thoughts and conversations surrounding homeschooling and homeschooling issues. While homeschooling is very important to me, in the end it is still a temporary part of my life. My relationship with Christ is eternal, and I want others to know that Jesus is the first priority in my life. I want to woo and win people with the attractiveness of Christ not necessarily the attractiveness of homeschooling.

My second realization concerned the homeschooling mold into which I was forcing myself. When my every spare moment is spent immersing myself in homeschooling activities, I run the risk of losing who I am as a whole person not simply a homeschooler. God has given me a passion for so many topics. I love history, cooking, tennis, baseball, mystery stories, writing, counseling, and so much more. As I focus exclusively on homeschooling, I begin to lose my passion for the other loves of my life.

Besides limiting my own personal growth, my unnatural focus on homeschooling provides a negative example for my children.

As I was encouraging them to explore and investigate everything that interested them, I was doing just the opposite, focusing on one subject exclusively. That day, I committed to pursue all the loves that God has placed in my heart. Obviously, one of those loves is homeschooling, but it is not the only love that draws my attention.

Broadening my horizons has had such a positive impact on our family. For me, I approach homeschooling more eagerly when it is not my sole focus. For the children, they have been encouraged and challenged by watching me continue to grow and learn. Whether it's a Bible study that I am completing or a new cookbook I'm reading, they are excited to talk to me about what I am learning. Instead of our conversations continually being teacher to child, often they become lively discussions between learners.

We can help ourselves not to become too focused on our homeschooling by taking the time to cultivate friendships with others who do not homeschool. If all of our social interactions are with homeschoolers, three guesses what the conversation will inevitably surround…homeschooling! Find friends who feed the other passions of your heart. I have several friends who love teaching Bible studies. What a joy it is to spend time with them sharing what we are learning as we teach others.

Along the same lines, may I encourage you to use your teaching gifts (You are a homeschool teacher, after all.) to invest in the life of a younger brother or sister in Christ? It's easy to get into a predictable rut of teaching our own children the Bible and spiritual concepts, but it is stretching to enlarge that teaching to encourage someone else. I'm not talking about teaching someone how to be a homeschooler, but instead, helping a younger believer grow in his or her own relationship with the Lord. Planning what to teach, sharing a common devotional time, and memorizing scripture together with your "student" will keep your own walk with the Lord vibrant and growing. My children have always loved the younger women with whom I spent time investing in the Word. It has been a great encouragement to them to see me sharing Biblical concepts with others and several of my older children are already spending time mentoring their own friends.

I want my children to become lifelong learners. My example is one of the most powerful tools I have to communicate the importance of lifelong learning. What are you passionate about? Invest in learning right alongside your children, and you will all reap the benefits!

# X

**I will give thanks to Thee, for I am fearfully and wonderfully made; Wonderful are Thy works.**

Psalm 139:14

# eXploration

Are your children explorers? I know mine are! They love to dig, turn over rocks, make art projects, and take apart appliances. For a wannabe neat freak like me, sometimes their exploration seems simply to be an avenue to more dirt on the floor and stains on their knees. When all eight of the children were at home, their explorations could ruin the day for me. I'm thankful God has continued to stretch me in this area by teaching me to facilitate their explorations. With only three children left at home, I'm envisioning the day my house stays clean, and I do not at all like the picture that conjures in my mind. Now I'm actively encouraging my little boys to dig and get dirty, and I sure wish I had been more excited about the older kids' dirt when they were still here!

How can we facilitate exploration in our homeschooling? Again, this is an area where studying your unique children will provide the answer to the question. For different children, different tools are

135

necessary to feed their hunger for exploration. As food for thought and to spark your imagination, let me share some of our "exploration supplies."

My daughter, Katie, has always loved to create in an arts and crafts type of way. Of course, I'm the exact opposite! I didn't automatically think about craft supplies regardless of what all the homeschool books recommended. However, once I realized just how much Katie longed to create, it became my responsibility to provide her with resources. To fill her crafting need, I invested in clear boxes and filled them with glue, scissors, beads, construction paper, pipe cleaners, Popsicle sticks, feathers, googly eyes, yarn, rickrack, and more. Next, I purposefully closed my eyes to the mess that Katie made as she was creating her masterpieces. Oh yes, you better believe I taught her how to clean up after herself as well, which made the whole occasion much more palatable for me.

Peter, as you can guess, liked to explore with film and sound. I provided him with cameras, tape recorders, and sheets and towels to make backdrops. The hardest part with Peter was watching him use delicate and expensive equipment as a young boy. Everything in me wanted to shout, "No, you might break it!" Fortunately, my husband reins me in and forces me to take my controlling hands off situations like that. With each opportunity, Peter became more and more proficient, and soon he was using his own money to buy equipment. It's funny, but now that he's an adult and in charge of thousands of dollars worth of equipment, he seems much more careful!

Emma loved to decorate the enormous dollhouse her father had built for the girls. Helping her to explore her interests meant providing fabric and pretty scrap booking paper for her to create rugs, wall hangings, curtains, and other "useful" dollhouse items. True confession: I had a picture in my mind of how perfectly the dollhouse should be decorated, and Emma's vision of perfection and mine didn't exactly match. Thankfully, I didn't even need Steve to stop me that time; I knew I just needed to keep my ideas to myself!

Molly was my dress up queen. She loved to make historical outfits and designed a vast wardrobe out of the hand-me-down formals I gave to her. I spent a little money at the thrift store and filled a large box with shoes, gloves, hats, dresses, and shawls. One Christmas, I gave the girls my wedding dress and veil as a Christmas gift. Molly loved that dress and spent many a school day adorned as a bride.

Nate loved to build towns, forts, and wooden furniture. For him, the supplies for exploration consisted of a toolbox full of screwdrivers, hammers, nails, wrenches, and a saw. We also provided him with an axe and careful instructions about how to use it safely. Nate spent hours in the garage building with his father's scrap lumber.

For Baleigh, ever since she was small, keeping up with her friends has been her love. I provided Baleigh with her own scrapbook and allowed her to use my scrapbooking tools to create her scrapbook pages. She was the only one of my girls to take up rubberstamping cards as well. Providing Baleigh with supplies to explore her interests simply meant sharing what I already owned. Now, to be completely honest…Yes, I owned those supplies, but I never really used them. I was coerced, through guilt, by several of my friends, to begin scrapbooks for each of the children. At that point, I already had seven children, and I was at least ten years behind in chronicling their lives. I think each scrapbook ended up with about five completed pages. That's just not who I am! I finally gave myself the freedom to quit. Now, I write, and my children will always have my books to remember what their childhoods were like!

Stephen loves baseball. He's always loved baseball. Exploration for him meant collecting baseball cards, reading about baseball players, setting up a pitching mound, and throwing lots of grounders. I've never met someone so single-minded about a sport. He knows who's who among the major league players and what their stats and highlights are after each game.

His hobby is one of the dirtiest (grass stains, anyone?), but the beaming smile on his face each and every time he has the opportunity to play is well worth the extra time I spend on laundry.

When Taylor was seven years old he took apart his first appliance and repaired it. Exploration supplies for Taylor consist of an electric set, pliers, screwdrivers, flashlights, WD-40, and the freedom to take things apart and put them together again. I must admit that I'm always a little nervous he'll electrocute himself or start a fire, but so far so good. My uncle allowed his son to do the same type of exploration, and I remember when he and my brother caused an explosion in the garage. My dad would have never allowed us to make that kind of mess, and I thought my uncle was awesome! I want Taylor to think I'm awesome too!

Take some time to consider what areas your children hunger to explore. Do they like to create, or craft, or bake, or memorize stats, or take pictures? Supplying them with what they need to explore those areas should be a high priority for your homeschool budget. None of what I provided for the kids cost an exorbitant amount, but it showed them that I was willing to do what it takes to help them learn about what they love.

Unless it's your child's idea, don't try to force them to turn their beloved hobby into a for-profit business. Let them enjoy what they are doing just for the joy it brings to their heart; having said that, some children just have a knack for turning their hobbies into a money- maker. More power to them! However, beginning a business can really change the dynamic of a much-loved activity, so be sure they understand the ramifications of what they're doing before they ever begin the process.

Messes happen! Just close your eyes to the messes in the moment! Provide your kids with supplies and adequate storage for those supplies. Then, teach them how to clean up after themselves. Display their masterpieces and "Ooh" and "Ahh" over their successes. Inquisitive children who are allowed to explore will become creative problem solvers as adults. What a wonderful opportunity we have to help them along the way!

# 𝒴

You shall not covet your neighbor's
wife, and you shall not desire your
neighbor's house, his field or his male
servant or his female servant, his ox
or his donkey or anything that
belongs to your neighbor.

Deuteronomy 5:21

# "You're Not Fair!"

As we spend our days homeschooling, it is fairly easy to see the major character flaws in our children's lives. I don't often miss a blatant lie. Disobedience and disrespect are easily recognizable and just as easily dealt with and corrected. However, there is one unhealthy character area that too often slips past me and rears its ugly head. I'm talking about the fairness trap. The mistaken idea our children hold onto so tenaciously, that life, and especially family life as it pertains to them, must be fair and equitable at all times.

As adults, we know this fact: Life isn't always fair. It's important for our children to learn that fact as well. When we try to shield them by making sure that everything that occurs or is bestowed in

141

our homes is absolutely fair, we rob them of an important lesson, and we are planting their feet firmly on the road of entitlement. Fairness and coveting go hand in hand. From the beginning, as far back as the Garden of Eden, our propensity as humans has been to covet and declare life as unfair. Satan merely insinuated to Eve that God was being unfair by withholding the fruit from the tree of the knowledge of good and evil from her, but that insinuation caused Eve to immediately covet what was not hers and the consequences of her coveting have been devastating.

Sometimes, we unwittingly teach our children to have huge expectations when it comes to fairness. Every time that we buy all the children a gift when it is one child's birthday, we are reinforcing the notion that fairness is a legitimate character quality. When we allow grumbling because one child received something that another child did not, we are perpetuating envy. When our children are offended because another child was praised when they were not, we are building habits of jealousy. Be careful what you are teaching in your home. Often, we are responsible for the negative fruit that is robbing our family of a good testimony for the Lord.

Coveting is an almost laughable sin. There are times that my children covet something they don't even like, for example, broccoli. Just because another sibling has it and they don't, suddenly they want it! Stay aware and be on the lookout for the fairness trap in your home. Our children need to learn to be happy for one another, not envious and covetous of one another. Coveting and the fairness trap happen in every home, but because we are together all day, every day, the opportunities for coveting are much more available. To be honest, when the children were all young, some days it seemed like all I did all day was remind them to be happy for one another. I wondered if they would ever get the lesson. What a joy it has been to see the positive fruit of that very repetitive lesson!

When our third daughter, Molly, was a little girl, she was sick all the time. I can't even record how many mornings I had to leave the other children home doing schoolwork while I took Molly to the doctor. She struggled through multiple cases of strep, three bouts with pneumonia, surgery to remove her tonsils and adenoids, sinus surgery, and an operation to remove a cyst on her eye. Because of her health problems, she naturally received more attention from her father and me.

Although the other children felt sorry for Molly, there was also a fair amount of grumbling about the unfairness of her extra time alone with us. For Molly, the doctor visits and surgeries were unwanted and unwelcome, but for the children left at home, they seemed like opportunities for extra attention from us and time off from school.

After one particularly troubling episode of grumbling and poor attitudes, my husband and I called a family conference. We asked Molly to tell the children how she felt physically most of the time. We talked about all of the extra activities that Molly missed because of her frequent illnesses. Then, we asked the children if it seemed fair to them that Molly was stuck at home, in bed, while they went to the library, to church activities, and to their friend's homes. We reminded them that we didn't allow Molly to complain when they had special outings, and that, generally speaking, she was happy for them. Then, we asked the children how they could show compassion to their sister rather than feeling jealous and covetous of her perceived special treatment. We didn't tell the children what to do, but we suggested that they work together to find ways to bless Molly.

That family talk was a real turning point for our children. Instead of grumbling when I left for the doctor with Molly, the children began to scheme and plot surprises to make her time of illness easier to bear. They would change her sheets so that she came home to a freshly made bed. They would find the portable DVD player and choose movies for her to watch in bed. They made little snack trays and filled pitchers with juice to keep by her bedside. They looked for quiet games they could play with her while she was lying down. They found ways to bless Molly, and in the process they were blessed themselves.

The real proof of their change of heart came last year. In Molly's sophomore year of college, she developed numerous lumps that the doctors feared were cancerous. Soon those lumps joined together to form a large mass. Whether it was cancerous, or not, without question the mass had to be removed. We arranged for her to have the surgery to remove the mass over her Christmas break from college. Because her doctors were in the state where she attended school, the surgery necessitated her and me traveling to South Carolina and staying in a hotel after the surgery was complete; an expensive proposition, but necessary to help Molly. My husband and I prayed about Christmas and how to afford gifts for the others, while still saving enough money for the trip south for Molly and me. One evening, several weeks before Christmas, our children announced a family conference. That's not a very common occurrence at our house. Normally, Steve or I will call a conference time, so since they called the conference this time, we knew the children had something important to say. At the conference, they told us that all they wanted for Christmas was for me to be able to travel with Molly. Instead of gifts, they wanted the money to be put toward hotel accommodations and meals. What a blessing, and what an affirmation that our children had really learned how to be happy for one another. As an added blessing, on Christmas morning they presented Molly and me with little presents to entertain us on the trip. Again, Molly was blessed, I was blessed, and so were they!

Don't grow weary when it comes to teaching into the fairness trap. As you train your children to be generous not envious, they will be learning important character qualities such as: compassion, commitment, humility, loyalty, self-control, and patience. There is nothing more winsome than children who care about others more than they care about themselves. That others orientation will make them shine as lights in a lost and dying world, and God will bless them as they seek to bless others.

This you know my beloved brethren.
But let everyone be quick to hear,
slow to speak and slow to anger.

James 1:19

# Zeroing In On Issues

## The Family Conference Table

I n the last section, as we looked at the fairness trap, several times I mentioned having a family conference. The Family Conference Table is a wonderful way to teach our children good communication skills and how to appropriately handle disagreement and discussion. Having the opportunity to call a Family Conference Table wherever and whenever we have need is a huge benefit of homeschooling.

Although our children sometimes believed The Family Conference Table was only used to address discipline issues, the Table is also a wonderful tool to involve the whole family in planning, goal-setting, and spiritual discussions. On the positive side, we often used The Family Conference Table to plan events such as our vacation. If it were up to me alone, our vacations would look very predictable and routine. By inviting the whole family to participate in planning our vacation, we ensured that everyone's ideas were heard, and that way ahead of time we understood what each family member was looking forward to on vacation. With that knowledge, we were then able to plan vacations that were enjoyable for everyone.

Sometimes, however, The Family Conference Table needs to be utilized to discuss issues that are bubbling under the surface in our home. There are times that I just can't put my finger on it, but something just isn't right in our family. Whether it is hidden sin or unresolved conflict, The Family Conference Table provides a safe venue to discuss the issues at hand.

The basis of The Family Conference Table is found in the book of Ephesians. In Ephesians 4:15 Paul says, "But speaking the truth in love, we are to grow up in every way into Him who is the head, even Christ." For The Family Conference Table to be an effective tool, it requires every family member to "speak the truth in love." Really, that verse breaks down into three very important components for The Family Conference Table. First, everyone must speak. In order for The Family Conference Table to accomplish a positive outcome, no one has the freedom to remain silent. Everyone must be involved in the dialogue. Silence can be a powerful and manipulative tool, and no family member should be allowed to use it to the detriment of others. Secondly, all involved must speak the truth. The Conference Table is not the place for embellishment or rationalizations. Each member of the family must commit to speaking the truth. Sometimes, the truth is hard to hear, but it is the third component of The Family Conference Table that makes the truth palatable. That third component is this: Family members must speak the truth in love.

The Family Conference Table is not the place for finger pointing or angry outbursts. The goal of The Family Conference Table is not to win an argument or be proven right. Rather, the goal is understanding, resolution, and reconciliation. Loving communication makes that goal much more attainable.

As we speak the truth lovingly, issues can be worked through in a calm and God-glorifying manner. Because everyone must speak at a Family Conference Table, even the youngest children have the opportunity to have their voices heard. Soon after initiating The Family Conference Table, Steve and I realized what a relief it was to the younger children to be able to share information that we might not be aware of without seeming to tattle on their older siblings. Because they were learning the proper way to share that information and because the other children were right there when it was being shared, the opportunity for misunderstanding and misinterpretation was alleviated.

An important aspect of The Family Conference Table is the necessity for those who have wronged others to be willing to admit their wrongdoing and seek forgiveness. I have had to learn to lead by example in this area. It is humbling to call a Family Conference Table to discuss the children's behavior issues, and then upon discussion to realize that it is my own poor attitude or impatience that is causing the problem in the first place. Unless I am willing to humbly seek my family's forgiveness, the only lesson they will learn is that mom can never admit she is wrong.

Whether the family conference is called for problem solving or goal setting and planning, we always include a time of prayer at the conclusion of each family conference. Especially when we have been discussing difficult subjects or conflicts, the prayer serves to draw our family close together in unity. Without fail, when we end a Family Conference Table the atmosphere in our home is light-hearted and sweet. Before closing in prayer we always make sure there are no more issues to be discussed, so when the prayer is completed we all walk away feeling restored and often relieved.

I grew up in a home that had more than its fair share of conflicts. How I wish my family had known how to resolve conflict through the peaceful use of The Family Conference Table. Instead of damaged relationships left to fester because of harsh words or the silent treatment, we could have learned to discuss issues, seek forgiveness, and start anew with fresh resolve to find closeness in our relationships. Because I so clearly realize what I didn't have growing up, I am completely committed to making sure my children realize that their relationships can be sweeter through learning how to communicate quickly, clearly, and with love.

Don't allow unresolved conflict to build and pile up in your home! Taking time away from schoolwork to resolve problems is a much more important lesson than any textbook can ever provide for our children. As they learn to communicate with honest and loving speech, you will be paving the way for solid relationships for them today and into the future.

# Afterword

## by Steve Scheibner

The decision to homeschool our children was not an easy one. In fact back in 1991, homeschooling was still illegal in many states and highly discouraged in most of the rest; however, in Pennsylvania, where we lived at the time, homeschooling was legal and taking on popularity among many in our social circle. Megan and I knew some homeschooled families, and we were impressed with what we saw. The children of those homeschooled families were clear-eyed, articulate, and generally delightful to be around. So, because of the inspiration those home-schooled children provided, we began to consider homeschooling as a viable option to the government-run school alternatives.

Before our first child turned five, Megan and I started looking into what it would take to educate our children at home. As we talked to other home educators and read articles, books, and publications about home education, most of our objections faded away. We learned that on average, homeschooled children score in the 87th percentile academically, a full 37% above their public school counterparts. Most home-educated children are mature for their age. They can hold a conversation with an adult and still play nicely with other children their age; however, not everybody was pro-homeschooling in those days. The NEA (National Education Association) excoriated homeschooling. Each year at the NEA national convention, the first item of business would be to officially condemn homeschooling as part of their national platform. Countless articles were written about the pitfalls of home education and the damage that would ensue due to lack of socialization. Not to mention my mom. She was dead set against us educating the children at home and didn't mind telling us that with each chance she got. Despite what I read from "so-called" education experts and my mother's objections, I clearly recognized that homeschooled children were not social misfits, unless you put maturity, integrity, honesty, consideration, courage, and academic achievement in the social misfit category. After considering all of the differing points of view regarding home education, we were ready to make a decision. Just to be sure, Megan and I prayed about the decision and felt peaceful and even led of the Lord to give homeschooling a try. Now, armed with a desire to rear character-healthy children who were mature, kind, and academically superior, Megan and I made the decision, jumped in with both feet, and enrolled our five year-old daughter Kaite in the local Christian school. Yep, that's right, we flinched. Much to the delight of my mother, who was known for saying, "He who hesitates is lost." We enrolled our little cherub in plan "B."

So, like dutiful parents straight out of a Currier and Ives scene, we walked little Kaite to the bus that early September morn and waved as the bus shrank into the morning mist. Then, as we turned and walked back to the house, that still small voice inside of me started yelling, "Way to go Einstein!" There is nothing like a good compromise to get the old second-guessing going, but for the time being I was able to put down the nagging doubts from within me and settle in for the long haul.

It didn't take long for Megan and me to see that plan "B" was not the best choice for our little Kaite. After just one week at school, we began to sense her pulling away from the family. Pleasing peers and teachers seemed to be more important to her than pleasing Mom and Dad. She began to refer to herself in the third person. She began to refer to the other children as "The Other Children."

She suddenly put on a superior attitude toward us and her siblings. Natural, I supposed, for a firstborn female; altogether understandable, actually, for a fifteen-year old girl. But wait! We didn't have a fifteen-year old; we had a five-year old! So the small voice within me grew increasingly adamant. Back and forth went the internal conflict. "Give the Christian school more time." "No, no, pull her out now before she pulls away from your authority altogether." So what were we to do, stay the course or sound retreat? And then came that fateful day when the impending decision to disenroll her came to a tipping point.

The school was trying to raise money to bridge the budget shortfall by conducting a magazine subscription drive. That's when our little impressionable kindergartener came home from school with her very first Metallica album on cassette. It seemed she had earned the heavy metal prize as one of the top sellers of magazines for the school. Now, I had the unfortunate task of wrestling the prized possession from the winner's death grip. Not even really sure what a cassette tape was and having no clue who or what the 80's heavy metal movement was all about, our precious daughter had bonded instantaneously with her precious prize. Yikes! Now, the small voice within me was in full-blown megaphone mode. So, I called the principal and asked for a meeting. He agreed, and the next day Megan and I met with him in his office. He started the meeting by quickly apologizing for some of the questionable magazine selections in the subscription drive. He seemed relieved, but puzzled, when we told him that we were not there to talk about the magazines; but that we were more concerned about some of the prizes being handed out, including the Metallica album in question. He appeared genuinely surprised regarding our concern about the music. He said he had no control over the prizes being offered, and then the words that set the next twenty years of our life in motion… "Besides, Kaite picked the prize herself, and you know… you are the first parents to have a problem with Metallica as a choice of prizes." Wow! What a moment of clarity. At that point, Megan and I stood up, shook his hand, and thanked him for his time. We then proceeded to remove her from that character-hostile environment, immediately enrolling her in the Cherryville Christian Academy, which was the name that we gave our first family homeschool based in Cherryville, Pennsylvania.

Megan knew all along that the Christian school alternative was not right for our family, but sometimes I come to the party late. Such has been the story of my life. She has been patient with me over the years. Since Megan is the primary day-to-day teacher in our homeschool (as most women are), she is the one that bears the burden of success or failure the most. I think most men would be inclined to let the kids run wild until they reached the age of thirteen or so, and then they would try to sell them to traveling Bedouins and call it good. My role has been more of a supporting one throughout the years. I have failed miserably from time to time in this role, however.

To illustrate what a flop I was at encouraging my wife in her role as the children's primary teacher, I must tell you about the trip to Israel. When our two oldest children were approaching middle school age, we traveled to Israel for one of those 10-day tours of the Holy Lands. (That trip also served as a perfect homeschool field trip.) After flying all night in a crowded 747 through JFK and on to Tel Aviv, we finally reached the hotel in Tiberius on the banks of the Sea of Galilee. Around 7p.m. local time and a full 30 hours after any of us had seen sleep, it was time to go through the buffet line at the hotel and finally eat a meal in something that was not moving. We sent the children through the buffet line ahead of us. As we enjoyed some fellowship back at the table, "it" happened. Peter came over to the table, sat down, and put his plate down in front of us. Smack dab in the middle of his enormous plate was a fish. You know, the European variety, head, scales, fins, the works, including the eyeballs! So, what was a father to do? I did what any other sleep deprived male would do at that moment, I said, "What is thaaat!" To which my nine-year old son said, "Chicken!" with total assurance. I think I muttered something under my breath about him being a moron, and I proceeded to tell him that. "That is one strange look-ing chicken." He doubled down and reiterated that it was most cer-tainly a chicken since that is what he asked for from the server in the buffet line. Ah yes, the source of our problem was the language barrier that somehow turned seafood into poultry. We all laughed, except for Peter, as I pointed him back toward the buffet line for a replacement chicken. This is when my thoughtfulness really shined brightly. Once Peter was out of earshot, I turned to my wife and jokingly whispered, "I don't think homeschooling is working!" She looked distressed but said nothing to me. Later that night is when the boulder I had dropped on her at dinner literally rolled over to crush me in bed. About two hours after my head hit the pillow, I woke up to the sounds of my wife sniffling. Apparently, she had taken the homeschooling comment to heart and was feeling like a failure. Who knew?? Not me for sure! What was a little pebble of a comment to me was a huge boulder of a comment for her. As we sat and talked about my inconsiderate comments, I realized that night that my role as the encourager-in-chief was an important one for my marriage, our children, and ultimately, the success of our homeschool.

Now, we have been at this thing called homeschooling for more than twenty years. We have experienced some wonder-ful highs and some discouraging lows, but through it all we have grown. Not just the children but Megan and I, as well. As I read the chapters my children sent us for the ending of this book, I laughed, I reminisced, and at points found myself choking back tears. God has indeed been good to us and I wouldn't trade our years of home-schooling for all the tea in China!

# Bonus Chapters
# The Children Speak!

*With*

Kaitlyn Elizabeth Thayer

Peter Warren Scheibner

Emily Marion Smock

Margaret Hannah Scheibner

Nathaniel Pierce Scheibner

Baleigh Grace Scheibner

Stephen Paul Scheibner, Jr.

Taylor Christian Scheibner

*and*

Katie Emerson

# Kaite's Story

"And the wild things roared their terrible roars and gnashed their terrible teeth and rolled their terrible eyes and showed their terrible claws." When I was young, well younger than I am now, I remember my dad reading this book to us before bed. He would roar, roll his eyes, gnash his teeth, and make claws with his hand. I would sit transfixed, listening and believing every word. Such is the power of a book and the magic of listening to one read out loud.

My memories of when I was little include many fun activities, action-filled days, and lazy nights. However, the best memories are the ones of people reading to me and of me reading a book to myself. I remember my grandpa's deep voice reading Little Black, a Pony and Romeo and Juliet, and my nanny lending her voice to the evil witch from Hansel and Gretel. Both of my parents read out loud to us. Dad read funny books such as: Dr. Seuss, Where the Wild Things Are, Nate the Great, and other shorter books.

My mom, though, she read books that have shaped me and influenced my life choices. I remember my mom reading every day, not just to us but also taking time to sit down and read a book to herself. Seeing my mom passionate about a book or a character in a book, encouraged me to want to read and helped me to want to relate to the story. Books such as The Chronicles of Narnia and The Hobbit gave me a love for fantasy. Little House on the Prairie and Leif the Lucky gave me an appreciation for our history and the trials that many have gone through. Aesop's Fables and The Book of Virtues taught me how to apply a story to my life and learn lessons from imaginary characters.

When I first learned how to read it didn't come easily, but I had a drive to learn. I wanted to travel to Narnia faster than my mom was reading out loud. I needed to know how the stories ended. I was the kid who would try to stay up late to just read one… more… chapter. That's still me! My parents didn't need to make me read; I wanted to read. Reading was a way to escape my world for just a minute; to see and experience new things, even if it was just in my imagination.

Books draw you in and enchant you. I would get so caught up with a book or a character that everything else was just not important. The first book I remember crying about was Baby. To this day I still tear up when Sophie comes to the funeral. The last book I cried over was Mockingjay. My poor husband just sat there with no clue what to do while I sobbed with the heroine. Good books are meant to draw on our emotions, to make us laugh, cry, to feel anger, love, fear, or hope. A great book you carry with you for years and read over and over again. I have a few books that are so loved that they fall open to my favorite parts and the characters feel like old friends when I think of them.

I honestly don't know what I would do if I didn't have books in my life. Ever since I could, I've been reading to myself and out loud to others. When I read to myself I soak up the books like a sponge. When I read to others, I get drawn into the books, giving voices and feelings to characters. When we traveled on long road trips my parents would get books on tape, and we would listen to them instead of watching a movie or listening to music. When we got older, I would read out loud on the trips.

Books give you a way to expand your imagination, to explore different sides of your own character, and to challenge what you believe in and why. When you pick up a book, don't just settle for a happy book with no conflict. Instead, get a book that challenges you in some way; whether it challenges your beliefs, or your imagination, or the way you view the world and the people around you. Find hero's you want to be like, people who have something you don't, or who emanate a trait you would love to possess, or who have the courage to stand up in impossible situations. Ask yourself constantly whether this person is someone you want to be like or if they're someone you don't want to be like. We can learn from both types of characters; so don't just read books where the heroes are all alike. Challenge your idea of what a hero looks like; some run in with a sword, some are soft spoken peace seekers, some are antagonistic, some are meek, some you love, and some you love to hate, even when they do the right thing.

A love of reading is important to impart to your children at a young age. I work as a nanny, and last year when the triplets were 5 and the other was 3, I read The Lion the Witch and the Wardrobe, out loud to them. Ever since they have lived and breathed the story. They have each claimed a character from the four Pevensie children (I'm the White Witch) and have aspired to be just like them. Who wouldn't want their child to seek to be valiant, just, gentle, and magnificent? And that is just what these four are doing. Asking if their actions are like those of their character in the book, desiring to be good kings and queens, believing completely in a land called Narnia, and that good will always wins in the end even when it seems that it won't. The two oldest girls are now avid readers like me, especially the oldest. I often find her curled up in a corner with a chapter book. The latest and greatest to her is The Hobbit, and you have to drag her away for eating or bedtime. Even then, she'll ask for me to read out loud during dinner or before bed. Teaching your children to love reading and to understand what they are reading will open so many doors for them. I am thankful to the adults in my life that helped instill a love of books in me when I was young, and I plan on doing the same for my children and the children in my care.

# Peter's Story

**B**eing asked to write the afterword for your English teacher's book is simply not fair. There is the initial pressure of, "What do I write?" followed by the knowledge that you need to avoid all of the grammatical errors that she has ever hounded you for. Throw into that the fact that I was homeschooled, so corporal punishment wasn't completely out of the question, and you have a recipe for disaster. All that said it is a tremendous honor to be writing for my mom's book. I remember the first year that Katie went to kindergarten and I went to preschool. We left early in the morning. I played with friends and got back just in time for a nap. Katie was home when I got up. We had dinner, played for an hour, and then it was back to bed to start all over the next day. Looking back, I realize now what I couldn't have realized then: I missed my family. The time that we had together was always short and punctuated by bed. I don't remember the conversations that led my parents to decide to homeschool, but I can imagine looking back now that they simply didn't want my childhood to be a series of memories that would have been shaped by others and filled in by them. The greatest gift I have been given by my family is simply that: the gift of family. I knew who I was. I was a Scheibner, and I didn't want to be anything else.

Homeschooling taught me a great deal of valuable lessons. I learned that if I started my work earlier, I would get done sooner. I found that if I worked ahead I could take time off later. I discovered that if I didn't treat my sisters respectfully then all that I would get to do for the rest of my life was school. However, there is one lesson that I never really was able to master (or even fake my way by), and that was the "Log." Someday I'm sure that somebody will try and analyze why I didn't ever (and I do mean EVER) fill out my logbook. Honestly, it wasn't rebellion, forgetfulness, or disobedience. It was simply that I didn't ever make the point to fill out my log. And let me tell you, if you wanted to see Peter break into a cold sweat all you had to do was say, "Peter, bring me your log please." As soon as those words would exit my mother's mouth I would become like a caged animal. I would run to my room and freakishly attempt to fill in the missing information. My mother would eventually walk up to my room and catch me in the act, and I would again be grounded for the rest of my known existence. I never did get over this mental block with the log, and to this day I still have trouble laughing when everybody else at the table is recounting my many misfortunes. I write this not to say that I learned a valuable lesson, so much as to say that homeschooling is tough. As my wife and I have started to have children of our own and are making choices about how we raise our family, I can look at this period and realize that there are some battles that just have to be fought, even if there is no victory in sight. I did learn many lessons through the log, however: The need to be responsible for my own work, bookkeeping, the fastest route to getting grounded, and, eventually, how to own up to my mistakes and take personal responsibility for my actions (or in this case inactions). I do have to admit, I was truly crestfallen when I found that my mother (in her infinite wisdom) no longer made the children fill out their own logbooks. I guess they have me to thank.

Peter Scheibner, paving the way to a better, log-free future.

Now, I must admit that I didn't always see eye-to-eye with my family. Emma and I had the sibling rivalry thing down to a science. For instance, when I was ten I had a very impressive pumpkin patch. In the middle of my patch was the prize pumpkin. I truly cared for this pumpkin. I got up early in the morning to inject the stem with milk. I pruned any excess growth near this particular pumpkin. I obsessed over the condition of the soil surrounding the mound. After an entire season my pumpkin was over 4 feet in diameter, and our next-door neighbor had basically promised me that I would win the county fair if I decided to enter. One morning in late August I awoke to a tragedy in the patch. Emma had risen earlier than normal, retrieved a sharpened stick, walked out to my pumpkin, and riddled it with stabs. There wasn't a 3-inch section that hadn't been punctured. I'm not sure if I will ever fully get over the heartbreak.

But one of the best parts of being at home with your siblings basically every day of the week is that you really get to know them well. I can sit down with any of my comrades in crime and recount past glories, plan future escapades, or just ask them what the Lord has been teaching them. I know who they are and what motivates them. And better than that, I care. For years Emma and I were the only two who just couldn't get along. It could have been the pumpkin thing, but I actually think my mother was right on this one. We were just too much alike. We were outgoing, incredibly smart and quick-witted, very competitive, and easily offended by the other. When we had fun together, we had more fun that two people should be allowed. When we fought, we shook the house with our fury. This was the model for our relationship until we went to college. I had already attended one year of college in Florida but had decided to transfer to Bob Jones University for my sophomore year. Emma had separately decided to go to Bob Jones, as well, the same year. All of a sudden, Emma and I found ourselves together at the crossroads of our lives. From this point on Emma and I have basically crossed life's many bridges at the same time. The first year of school, Emma and I saw very little of each other. It wasn't that we were avoiding one another, but our paths never really crossed. When they did, Emma was usually with her friends from Culinary who didn't think too fondly of me. In fact, it became very difficult to be around her because whenever I was I became the automatic butt of every joke. It seemed that nothing had changed in our relationship until the end of the year. One evening, I saw Emma sitting on a bench looking somewhat out of sorts. To anybody passing she would have appeared to just be studying, but I could tell right away that something was wrong. When I sat down next to her she quickly poured out that there was a boy who had been texting her lewd things, and she didn't know what to do. I found out all of the information that I could, and then told her that I would go with her to the Dean of Men to report the issue. I stayed with her through the whole ordeal. This was one of the first times that Emma and I had to fix a problem without the help of our parents. We saw in the other a confidant and a friend. From that point on we were thicker than thieves. We started dating our future spouses at about the same time. I got married just a few months before she did. She started a career job just weeks before I got my offer. Through all of the big decisions that life has thrown at us, we have always been able to go to the other and get honest, frank, humorous, yet always God-focused counsel. Everybody knows that Baleigh (the youngest girl in the family) is my "favorite," but Emma and I are the closest. We always seem to know what the other person needs, even if they wouldn't accept it from anyone else.

If you are considering homeschooling your family, I have just a few things that I would warn you of and offer my counsel, if you would be willing to accept it. Don't homeschool purely for the academic advantages. Yes, homeschoolers usually win the national spelling bees and traditionally score higher on standardized tests than their public-schooled counterparts, but if you, as a parent, push your child they will succeed academically wherever you put them. If you are considering homeschooling just because everybody else in your local church does, don't do it. Fads come and they go. It will be a better service to your children to have some consistency in their education than to be in a home setting one year and in a private school the next, only to be shuffled to a public school in the end. Homeschooling should be viewed as a tool, and if you are going to use it, use it to build a family identity. Homeschool your children so that you may have their hearts. Teach them diligently how to love their siblings, interact with adults, self-motivate, but most importantly, to build a family identity. I am a Scheibner, and there is nothing else I'd rather be.

# Emma's Story

What I liked about homeschooling:

There were many things that I enjoyed about homeschooling. One is that if I worked hard and got my school done in the morning, I would still have time for play. I was a very active child and sitting still for schoolwork was often boring.

I liked working in our garden in Pennsylvania. It was educational as well as fun. I was in charge of growing the zucchini, and when they were ripe Mom taught me how to make muffins and bread. I think this is what started my love for cooking. I also liked being able to help my little siblings with their schoolwork. I taught my youngest brother Taylor how to read, and I helped Stephen learn how to do multiplication. I think it builds a closer bond when you are helping each other to learn and grow. I liked that I could learn at my own pace. If a subject came easily to me, I could get through it quickly, but if I was struggling with anything… math… I could go slower and take my time. There was never a rush to get through a subject because the point was to learn it well not to meet a deadline.

I liked going on different field trips. I remember one time when we went to an old fort in Maine and got to spend the day walking around and learning about the history of the people who lived there. I also remember when we went to Washington, DC for the day and all the museums that we got to see. My favorite part was seeing Julia Child's kitchen. The counters were so tall because she hated having to bend over all the time.

My older brother Peter and I got ourselves into all sorts of trouble. We would read about some war or battle in our history text, and then we would pretend for the rest of the afternoon that we were there. Quite a few bruises came from that, but also a lot of really great memories. We would also encourage each other to keep reading. When we were in high school, he and I made a deal that if I read three books that he picked for me, he would have to go spend money on clothes that I picked out for him. This worked out great for both of us. He got some really nice clothes, and I got to read the Count of Monte Cristo.

When we were living in Pennsylvania, Peter and I would get up early and make some Lipton tea, putting in ridiculous amounts of sugar. We would talk and do our devotions and then get started on our schoolwork. I don't think that either of us liked having to be inside all day, so we always tried to finish school before lunch.

## What I did not like about homeschooling:

I am very easily distracted, and with so many people in the house it was easy to just not focus. On the days I got distracted, I always ended up still in the schoolroom late into the afternoon and evening.

## How homeschooling helped Pete and me:

Peter and I are so much alike that we often did not get along. He was annoying, and I was headstrong. We were always trying to out-do each other. I will never forget the time that he made me so mad I went and stabbed the pumpkin that he had been growing for the fair. Now, that was bad, and he was so upset and hurt, but that was the way we treated each other. One thing that Mom and Dad always said to us was that our siblings should be our best friends. I never really thought that was true until we got to college. All through high school our parents tried to get us to work together and to learn to like each other. We had our good times, and we had some really bad times…. Looking back, I'm surprised our parents didn't kill us sometimes! Peter and I were freshmen together at Bob Jones University. It took awhile for me to realize that I really wanted to spend time with my brother. I really started missing him in the first semester of our second year, and we decided to set aside time every week to have a meal together. He helped me go through a very difficult time that semester. He was right there with me, and we grew so much closer through that experience. That year we both met our future spouses, and we would all hang out and play games. It was so much fun to be adults together! Now, his wife is my best friend, and he and I are so close.

## We like our traditions:

One thing that has always been true about my family is that we love our traditions. From the smallest things, like we hold our breath under every tunnel, to the big things, like where we spend our vacation and never waiting until Christmas to open presents, we can be counted on to keep with tradition. In some ways, I think these traditions are what make our family special. I can remember every year since I was 3, counting down to our vacation in Delaware. We always went to Bethany Beach, and for 17 years we rented the same house for the same three weeks. Mom would start counting in January, saying that we really only had "three months 'til vacation because you can't count the month you are in, and you can't count the month you go." never mind that she started counting January 1st and we didn't leave until May 29th. We would laugh and tease her for "funky counting," but we would count that way, too. We would go to a local pizza joint on our first night there, and that always made it seem like vacation was finally starting for me. Even after we moved to Maine, we made sure to go back to Bethany every summer. Many of us call it our favorite place on earth, even though it is just a little old beach town. It has some of the best memories for me growing up. I learned how to ride a bike there, and Dad would take anyone that could ride a bike to the boardwalk in the mornings and buy us a donut. We bike riders would sit and watch the seagulls on the beach.

One year we had to stay at a different house, and to be honest that vacation was not as fun. Not because we didn't do the same things, but because we weren't following tradition. Right when you drove into Bethany Beach there was this hideous totem pole. It had a face carved into it, and all the kids would yell, "Dad, look, it's you!" One year, the totem pole was removed because they had to do some work on it. That was the most disappointing drive into town. We would literally hold our breath waiting until we could see it so that we could yell at Dad… but it wasn't there, and we didn't get to keep with tradition. Thankfully, they restored it the next year, and I am happy to report that my dad's statue has been termite-free for several years now.

Dad had to fly a lot over the holidays when we were growing up, mostly over Christmas. We didn't mind that much because we would just have Christmas when he got back; however, that started the tradition of never opening presents on Christmas. As we got older, he had to fly less, and he would be home for Christmas. On Christmas Eve we would all get in our pajamas and watch White Christmas. Then, Dad would say, "Ok guys, we all get to open ONE present. Just ONE." So, we would gather around and pick the one present we wanted to open. After opening the first present, mom would say, "That's it… off to bed." To which Dad would reply, "Oh… I think we can open just one more… It is Christmas Eve after all." Soon all the presents were opened, and there was nothing left for Christmas morning except our stockings. After I got married, I tried to carry that tradition on to my new family… Yeah, but, they aren't as weak as my family. It's sad really.

## Your siblings are your best friends:

This statement is so true. There was never a shortage of friends growing up. I always had someone to play with. This someone was usually Molly. I got her into all sorts of trouble. We would try to stay up all night, or we would try to be helpful and clean the house. Just for the record, we were really good, sweet kids. Molly and I one day got the idea that Mom would love it if we cleaned the kitchen floor for her. We did have a mop, but we wanted the floor to be really clean. So we filled buckets with soapy water and got down on our knees and scrubbed away. Our parents came down half-way through our good deed and freaked out. Apparently, the floor was the kind that you can't get a lot of water on. You have to mop very carefully or the floor can bubble up. Well, it did just that, and though Mom and Dad tried to be nice about it, we could tell that they were not super happy with our cleaning. They still have not let us forget about it to this day. I'm not kidding! Mom brought it up again on the phone just this morning.

Of all my siblings, I am the closest to my baby brother. Taylor and I have a special bond. He was adopted, and Katie and Peter left for college only a few years later. That meant that I was Tate's second mommy. I taught him how to read, and I gave him baths. He would hit me, and for a while he really hated me, but after he got over that we became best friends. We always buy a box of Oreos and split them when I come home to visit. We talk and try to steal the other person's crème. I knew Taylor accepted my husband when he invited Steve to share in the sacred Oreo ceremony. No one, and I mean no one, is allowed to join us unless specifically invited.

These are the traditions and memories that I really cherish. It is what makes my family unique. It is the glue that keeps us together in a way. We may go through rough times, or we may fight, but there are always memories of the good times. We can always bring up some memory or tradition at home that makes us thankful for each other.

# Molly's Story

While many people would say that homeschooling is not a legitimate way of educating one's children, I would very much have to differ. Yes, homeschooling comes with its own advantages, such as: more free time, more field trips, and many, many more days off; but homeschooling still comes with its own set of challenges. My personal set of challenges came in the way of sickness.

Ever since I was a wee, little, adorable child, I have suffered with an immune system that thought it could live its own life instead of obeying my wishes and just staying healthy. This was, of course, very frustrating when every day I had different school lessons that need to be completed. Fortunately for me, my family was my number one Wellness Crew. I, Molly Scheibner, was the sickest member of the entire Scheibner clan. You name a sickness, and I have probably had it. Strep throat was a big struggle for me during high school. It seemed like every two weeks I was dealing with strep throat. Even though I was sickly most of the time, my family did a great job of getting me "set-up" when I got home from my doctor's visits. They would have my bed ready and some macaroni and cheese waiting for me along with a tall glass of ginger ale. I'm not hard to please, and that menu really hit the spot! Now to most people, that sounds like the life. Right? I mean how could it really get any better than that? Unfortunately, this was not some scene from a movie where the damsel in distress got to relax and enjoy her bounty. No, I still had a ton of school to do, whether I felt like it or not.

Now, the way that my mother laid out our school schedule was very easy to understand. I would have my different subjects every day, and I knew the number of pages that I would need to complete in them. Being the middle child also helped me, because whenever I was stuck on a particular subject, I could call for one of my older siblings to come and help me with it. I guess, for me, the most helpful part of homeschooling while I was sick was the utter silence. None of my family would come around me once I was locked away in my own room with my silly immune system and it's attitude problems. So, while I was all alone, I could finish my school quickly and have the rest of the time to rest or watch Shirley Temple movies. I felt bad for those kids in public or private schools who had to take a whole day off from school when they were really ill and then had to do their "makeup work" when they returned to the classroom. I know that personally, I would not have like the stress of having to go to school every day and then bringing homework home. I much preferred to just get all of my work done in a timely manner every morning. Sometimes, I would even work ahead in my lessons so that I could have a "day off" later in the week. So you see, as far as the sickness aspect goes, homeschooling really was a treat.

Now being sick and in bed all of the time is not the only aspect of homeschooling that involved me (although it sometimes seemed like it was). There was also the part of homeschooling that involved extra-curricular activities. I am a very social person and whenever I was not sick and at home, I liked to be able to go out and get involved in activities that either involved my other homeschooling friends or my very own siblings. I cannot remember a time when my brothers and sisters and I were not outside playing or busy building our wild forts in the woods. Homeschooling gave us that time in the afternoons when we could go outside and use our crazy wild imaginations. I remember the times that we would finish our school and go play Little House on the Prairie. I was always the youngest Ingalls child who did not get to talk too much. (You have no idea how hard that was for me!) Even though homeschooling comes with its own set of problems, I cannot think of any other way that I would have wanted to go through my school years. When I went to college, I missed sitting in the dining room to do my math. I missed having my mom write out my schedule for me. I missed our homeschool.

The last thing that I want to talk about is the chances I had to teach my own siblings. The Scheibner family is a team, and growing up we always put that into practice. I would help my younger brothers with their reading or my sister with her spelling just as my older siblings had helped me. We each had our own school subject in which we really excelled. For me it was spelling. I could out-spell anyone in my family. I remember when my mom use to pick out some really hard words for my sister and me to try to spell out, and we would see who could spell them out the fastest and get the most correct. I almost always won! Later, I was able to take my awesome spelling skills and use that with my younger siblings. Especially because I had some siblings that struggled with certain subjects, I was glad to be able to help them overcome their struggles. Because we were homeschooled, my mom was able to take the specific time each of us needed to work on our problem subjects, and for that I'm very thankful.

# Nate's Story

There were many pros and cons to being homeschooled. From not having to get up early to getting school done by twelve, the life of a homeschooler is not as stressed as those who go to public or private school.

Overall, I enjoyed my homeschool life. I got to be with my family, play outside in the woods, and learn at my own pace. Even though I did not spend a lot of time "socializing," I had lots of friends. I did other things to make friends such as being involved in church and playing on the tee ball team. I was not what you would call socially savvy, but that didn't matter to me. I had a loving family, and I loved them back.

When it came to schoolwork, I did the best I could. Math, Science, Spelling, English, Social Studies, History, I learned them all. The one subject I had the most trouble with was Reading. Reading did not come naturally to me. I struggled with how it all worked, none of it made sense in my head. Plus, it also became a source of fear for me.

One Sunday at church, the Sunday school teacher called on me to read a verse from the Bible to all the other kids. My dad was the pastor, and the other kids thought that I should know all the verses already. As I looked at the verse in the Bible, all sense left my head. I could not put two sounds together. I tried and tried, but I could not figure out the words on the page. Frustration turned to embarrassment as my friends started to laugh. Even though the teacher stopped them right away, they knew that I could not read. For about three years after that event, kids would come and shove a piece of paper in my face and ask me to read what was on it. I hated that, but I tried not to show my anger. Being homeschooled definitely didn't protect me from being ridiculed.

Eventually my mom and dad realized what was going on. They sent me to a training center called Sylvan Learning Center. For four or five months, the patient teachers at Sylvan taught me how to get around my reading problems. I learned how to pick up any piece of paper and read what was on it to the people around me. Even though this did help when I was around other people, it still didn't give me a love for reading. I could do it, but only because I had to. It was not until one year at Christmas when Mom got me the book Eragon that I learned to love reading. The book was written by a homeschooler, and so I started to read it. As I read about dragons and magical things that would blow your mind, I wondered about the other books my mom had gotten me over the years. Were they as exciting as Eragon? I began another book, then another, then another! Before I knew it, my mom was beginning to tell me that I had to put down my book and go outside for some exercise.

Even though I am not the best student out there, I believe that being homeschooled did not hurt me at all when I got to college. I am keeping steady grades and a good work ethic; both things I learned from being around my mom and dad. They taught me to always want better for myself and to do the best I could. There is a high degree of love in my family; we are not perfect, but we always will forgive one another.

The fact that I was not exposed to alcohol, drugs, sex, and a general disrespect for the majority of my day, I think has made me a better person. Think about it, if kids didn't have that stuff distracting them all the time, they would get better grades in school. But I digress. If I could go back and do it all over again, I would not change a thing. I learned much more than what the books taught me. I learned to think for myself. And that was my time as a homeschooler.

# Baleigh's Story

## Or
## Balancing My Life:
## "The Busy Life of a
## Homeschool Teen"

Yikes! The name of this chapter just makes me go into the "What do I need to do today to get everything done?" mode. Many people think that homeschooling is very easy and their view of us is basically that we stay in our pajamas all day and watch movies and just be lazy. I wish that were the case! My day, as of now, consists of getting up (That's the hardest part.), doing my chores, getting to my school, and getting it done as well as I can! Then, depending on the day, I either head off to swimming or SAT Prep class. (I'm not sure which is more fun... Sarcasm... Swimming is WAY more fun!) If sports were a subject, that would be what I would study in college.

Growing up I was probably one of the first to really want to do athletics. As a homeschooler, I wasn't sure if I would be able to do sports; however, my freshman year of high school I decided to try to join the swim team at the closest public school in Maine. I made the team and fell in love with swimming. It was hard at first to balance school and swimming at the same time, but after getting into a routine, I was able to balance school and swimming as well as my daily social schedule. Now, being in my senior year, I am the busiest I have ever been: balancing school, swimming, looking at where I'll go to college and what I will be studying (I've decided on Fashion Design.), as well as moving to a different state. Before I moved, my spiritual life was down in the dumps. I had little connection with God, and I didn't care to have one either. Now that I am in an environment where everyone loves the Lord, and they are super friendly, I have never felt closer to my Lord in all my life. It's amazing what He has done for me in the past couple of months!

Keeping up with my social life is challenging as well. (I know, right?! I'm not the socially awkward duck you all might think I am!) Many times I tend to pick my friends over my schoolwork, which I probably shouldn't do.... It's something I am constantly working on. Oh, by the way, did I mention I also have to get ready for prom? Yeah, that should be a subject all on it's own. So much work! Who knew there was such a thing as Homeschool Prom? Some people used to make fun of my siblings and me because we were homeschooled. It made me mad at times, but then I realized it didn't even matter because I was doing the exact same things they were doing, except at home! And I didn't have all the same social pressures that some kids have today. Sure, I still have temptations and struggles! My life is nowhere near perfect, and it's always a work in progress, but I am thankful that I have my mom and dad to push me and motivate me to do well in my academics and to strive to get good grades. Not only good grades, though, they also push me to be closer to God and to really seek Him out instead of waiting for Him to find me! I know for a fact that I would not be as motivated as

I am today without my mom and dad! I am also constantly balancing my relationship with God everyday, as well as school! He comes first and foremost in my life, but some days it's hard to put Him first; however, with the right training and motivation, it all works out! I would say the one thing that I don't enjoy about homeschooling is that sometimes I tend to procrastinate. Then, I end up hurrying to get my school done, and it isn't as well done as I would want it to be. That is about the only thing I don't like. If I could, would I go back and choose to attend public school? NO WAY! I enjoy life being homeschooled, and I intend to finish my senior year that way. Peace out, you all!

# Stephen's Story

I'm 14 years old and number seven of the eight Scheibners. I like baseball and all types of sports (other than golf). My favorite in the family is Peter. I enjoy going to church and going to school... sometimes. I hate long division. But none of these things define me.

Several things in my life have helped to make me who I am. Homeschooling is a big part of this because I've seen a lot of middle school kids, and I know that if I weren't homeschooled I'd be a lot like them. This year, though, I really wanted to go to a Christian school so I could have a new experience. I've always been homeschooled and wanted to try something different. But after thinking and praying about it, I decided homeschooling was my best option to learn more and still be a part of my parents' ministry. I'm grateful for the chance to be homeschooled so that I can travel with my parents, spend a lot of time with my siblings, and do sports.

Sports have changed homeschooling, though, because for a while I did a lot of sports and a lot less school. I had to figure out how to balance it. I was involved in basketball, baseball, swimming, soccer, and boxing all in the same year. There was one point where I would do boxing at 9 a.m., swimming at noon, and then baseball in the afternoon. I had to figure out how to get school in there, too. Eventually, I cut sports down to swimming and baseball. I knew I needed to get my school done, and to me, the other three sports were secondary. My advice would be, even though homeschooling allows you to have more free time, use that free time to do the things that are most important. I had to learn that school comes before sports and not all sports are of the same importance. It depends on what you're good at. If you're good at soccer, you should probably keep soccer as your primary sport. Even though I enjoyed soccer, basketball, and boxing, I wasn't as good at them as baseball and swimming.

Growing up in a big family was fun because I was the youngest for awhile. I was always spoiled by the older kids… and then Taylor showed up. He follows me around everywhere, and I've had to learn to live with it. Now, he's my best friend, and we do everything together. This year we're even on the same baseball team. Being the older brother, my mom had to talk with me about how to be a good influence for him. I'm still working on that today. When we're at baseball, there are a lot of times I want to tell him to find other friends to hang out with; but then I realize that I might be the friend he wants to hang out with. Our relationship is important to him, and it's a good opportunity for me to be a good older brother.

A big family makes Thanksgiving and Christmas fun. We get to sit around, tell funny stories, and make fun of each other. We've had to learn to laugh at ourselves as well as at each other. But there are times when having a big family complicates things. One time when we went camping, we were packing up to get ready to leave the campsite. I asked my dad if I could go to the bathroom before we left. He said, "Yes, make sure everyone goes to the bathroom before we leave." So I went to the bathroom, and when I came out everyone was gone. I had no idea where they were. They had left and forgotten I was in the bathroom. Luckily, our neighbors had gone camping with us, and they were still there. They gave me a ride back to our house. My family didn't even realize I was gone until our neighbors called them and told them I was with them. Evidently the car seemed pretty full, even without me!

Another word of advice: homeschooling is a great idea for kids, but just make sure you aren't excluding them from other activities. I've seen a lot of families who homeschool but don't get involved with sports, friends, or church. While each of these things can distract from school, like I said earlier, they are all good things. Once your priorities are balanced, things become a lot more relaxed and homeschooling is a lot more fun. As my dad would say, "Don't grow weary of doing well."

# Taylor's Chapter

I really like homeschooling. One of the best parts is that you always have somebody to talk to. If you are having a bad day, there is always somebody who can help. I'm always getting help with math from Stephen. He can pick out what I'm doing wrong and fix it. There is never a dull moment around the Scheibner house. My brothers and I have a lot of traditions when it comes to games. Peter and I like to play The BIGS on the Wii. Steve (Emma's "Thing") and I enjoy Monopoly. Nate and I would play keep-away. Stephen and I play baseball, football, soccer, tennis, Wii games, and anything and everything. The best part about being the youngest is that you learn what "not" to do from all of your older siblings. Seriously, those guys were always in trouble. Molly and Emma dumped water on the floor in the kitchen. Somebody, who will go unnamed, shot the TV screen with a BB gun. Peter rolled the truck. My siblings did a lot of really awful things. (At least I think they're awful!)

However, I could always count on them when I needed them. I had a car that I always carried around. It was a red Matchbox car that I really loved. One day, I was looking for my car, and I couldn't find it. I went to Mom and asked if she knew where it was. She responded with, "I don't know. Why don't you go and ask your siblings?"

And so the search for the red car began. We looked everywhere. I started in my room. I looked in the toy basket, under the bed, in the closet, behind the dresser, and basically everywhere. Everybody else had torn the house apart, but they were unable to find the car. In the middle of the search, I felt something in my pocket. I pulled it out and found my lost car was hiding in my pocket. I walked up stairs and proudly announced, "Probably, it was in my pocket." They didn't even get mad about all the time we had wasted. Everybody laughed, and we got back to school. What I really liked about home-schooling from this is that I always had a search party on hand, and we could all laugh together.

Everybody has been moving out recently. Peter and Emma were the first to move out. I wanted everybody to live together for-ever. After Peter and Rochelle got married, they came up to Maine to visit. I thought that they were moving in and got very excited. When they left I asked my Mom why they couldn't stay. The hardest part about being so close to your family is watching them leave. Someday I suppose that I'll have to move out too. But until then, I'm staying right where I am.

# Emerson's Chapter

[In the introduction, I shared that I was never comfortable with anyone following us around and observing our homeschooling. Katie Emerson, aka "Emerson," is the exception to that rule. We met Katie when she was a young single mom and the hostess at a local restaurant. Since we eat out fairly often, (My love language!) we quickly built a relationship with Katie. Soon, she was asking us questions about our family and our faith. We were thrilled when she accepted Jesus Christ as her personal Savior. Through a series of circumstances, Katie came to live with our family for eighteen months. She and her children didn't just live with us though; they became beloved members of our family. We jokingly call Katie our, "Not-A-Daughter," but truthfully, she is much more than a daughter. She has become a friend, a student, and a dearly loved sister in Christ. I think her story will be an encouragement to you. – *Megan Ann*]

Living with the Scheibners for eighteen months was quite the eye-opener. I had never given much thought to home-schooling, schedules, getting dressed just because you're up, or even cleaning as you go. All that changed when I witnessed how smoothly a household could be run with a solid foundation and a little effort. This was how I wanted to run my home someday, so I started taking notes!

I went to college to become a teacher, but the more I learned about the public school system the more I thought that I never wanted to send my own children to school. I didn't know the first thing about homeschooling, and I didn't even know where to start. After being at the Scheibner's for just a little while, I noticed how the kids were done with their school work in a timely manner, and they could get so much more done when they weren't a slave to the public school schedule. Megan could pick out their curriculum, which subjects they were going to focus on that year, and make it fun! I could tell this was something I wanted in the future for my children, but I didn't know if I could make it work. Little did I know that God had homeschooling in my family's future, and that He would work out every single detail.

Schedule, schmedule. At least that's what I thought when I had my first two babies. "They put themselves on a schedule; I don't need to do that. We don't need to plan out every day or every week. Let's just go with the flow." HA! Now that I've just had my fourth baby, I LOVE the schedule. My children thrive on their routines and sleep through the night. Well... mostly sleep through the night. We are still sleep-training the youngest one, and he's come a long way. If I didn't have a schedule, I don't know how I would function or even attend to my other children. Babies take up a lot of your time, especially when they are newborns, but having a feeding schedule and a routine for the other kids works out for everyone!

Megan taught me the importance of a schedule, and I'm so glad she did. I can get things accomplished around the house. I know when all my children are going to be asleep or having rest hour. I know when they are going to go to bed for the night, and I can hang out with my husband all by myself. We don't live and die by the schedule, but it sure is awesome to know what's ahead for the day and to plan accordingly.

When I lived with Steve and Megan, I was a college student and sometimes I would go to school in my pajamas. It was college after all, so why not be comfortable while sitting in class all day long? Every morning when I got up, whether it was a day I was going to school or a day off, Megan was always dressed. She had her shoes on, her hair done and makeup on, and she always looked so put together. This was every single day, it didn't matter if she had somewhere to go or not, she was always ready. She didn't have to be embarrassed if the UPS deliveryman came, or the neighbors stopped by, or she had to run to the store at the drop of a hat; she was prepared for her day, no matter what came at her.

On the other hand, I was a mess! I wore my 'lounge pants' (Let's not kid ourselves, they were jammies.) all the time. I was never ready for company. I would hide if anyone came to the door. I just looked messy. This was not how I wanted to be when I grew up. Now I get up just a little earlier and get ready for my day. I have my quiet time. I get dressed, even with my shoes on, and I do my hair and makeup. You can get so much more done when you are dressed in regular clothes. With just the simple act of getting dressed, you just feel more productive!

I love to bake. I haven't always known how to cook. When my first baby was born, I burned everything. A few years later when I had my second baby, I tried again, but this time, I started with baking. Every time I was in the kitchen, it looked like a tornado went through there. Sometimes I would clean up my mess; other times I would be in such a hurry, that I wouldn't have time to get the kitchen clean, so someone else would have to clean after me. One day I was given some advice about cleaning as I go. I could do some dishes as the oven was going or wipe off the counter as I was waiting for something to cool. This advice has been carried with me into my own kitchen. On the days that I don't clean as I go, I have a disastrous mess to clean up after dinner or whatever meal I'm making. When I clean as I go, it's not so daunting! I just have a few plates and forks to clean up and I can go to bed knowing that I'm going to wake up to a clean kitchen. What a great feeling!

The life lessons I learned while living with my 'family' are priceless. I am so thankful for the year and a half that I got to spend living and learning how to run a successful household. My house is by no means perfect, but I know that if I hadn't learned how to set a schedule, get homeschooling off to a great start, get dressed every day, or to clean as I go, we would live in a much more chaotic home. I love that my children can stay home and learn the topics that my husband and I find important. It's a wonderful feeling getting up to a clean house and not feeling like I'm starting out behind. Getting dressed in the morning has made me more productive, and I'm not hiding in my room if someone stops by unexpectedly. I will always be grateful to Steve and Megan and all their children for allowing me the opportunity to live with them and for teaching me the importance of family and balance and what it means to run a mostly smooth home.

# Stuff to Make Life Easier

## (Resource List...)

# BOOKS WE LOVE TO READ

Obviously, reading and books are an important part of our homeschooling day. Below, you'll find some of the books that we have loved; books that we've returned to over and over. I hesitate to put ages with books, since reading ability and age are so variable. Although there are some wonderful books that have been written in recent years, in general, I find that the older books do a more thorough job of clearly presenting good and evil. As well, while there are certainly exceptions to this rule, older books tend to have less questionable material. With newer selections, I try to take time to peruse the book myself, before passing it off to my children.

# READING RESOURCES

## Read Aloud:

Good Night Moon  — Margaret Wise Brown

The Runaway Bunny  — Margaret Wise Brown

The Little Fur Family  — Margaret Wise Brown

The Little Fisherman  — Margaret Wise Brown

Time of Wonder  — Robert McCloskey

One Morning in Maine  — Robert McCloskey

Make Way For Ducklings  — Robert McCloskey

Blueberries For Sal  — Robert McCloskey

The Steadfast Tin Soldier  — Hans Christian Anderson

The Very Busy Spider  — Eric Carle

The Very Clumsy Click Beetle  — Eric Carle

The Very Hungry Caterpillar  — Eric Carle

The Very Lonely Firefly  — Eric Carle

The Very Quiet Cricket  — Eric Carle

Mike Mulligan and His Steam Shovel  — Virginia Lee Burton

Katy and the Big Snow  — Virginia Lee Burton

The Little Engine That Could — Watty Piper
The Relatives Came — Cynthia Rylant
Caps For Sale — Esphyr Slobodkina
The Story About Ping — Marjorie Flack

## Early Readers:

Tacky The Penguin — Helen Lester
Little Black a Pony — Walter Farley
A Fly Went By — Mike McClintock
"B" Is For Betsy — Carolyn Haywood
Betsy and Billy — Carolyn Haywood
Back To School With Betsy — Carolyn Haywood
Betsy and the Boys — Carolyn Haywood
Betsy's Little Star — Carolyn Haywood
Betsy and the Circus — Carolyn Haywood
Betsy's Busy Summer — Carolyn Haywood
Betsy's Winterhouse — Carolyn Haywood
Snowbound With Betsy — Carolyn Haywood
Betsy and Mr. Kilpatrick — Carolyn Haywood
Pollyanna — Eleanor H. Porter
Betsy — Tacy — Maud Hart Lovelace
Betsy — Tacy and Tib — Maud Hart Lovelace
Betsy and Tacy Go Over the Big Hill — Maud Hart Lovelace
Betsy and Tacy Go Downtown — Maud Hart Lovelace
Heaven To Betsy — Maud Hart Lovelace
Betsy In Spite of Herself — Maud Hart Lovelace
Betsy Was a Junior — Maud Hart Lovelace
Betsy and Joe — Maud Hart Lovelace
Betsy and the Great World — Maud Hart Lovelace
Betsy's Wedding — Maud Hart Lovelace
Nancy Drew series — those copyrighted prior to 1980

The Hardy Boys series — copyrighted prior to 1959
The Bobbsey Twins series — copyrighted prior to 1979
The Boxcar Children series — Gertrude Chandler Warner
All of a Kind Family — Sydney Taylor
All of a Kind Family Downtown — Sydney Taylor
More All of a Kind Family — Sydney Taylor
All of a Kind Family Uptown — Sydney Taylor
Ella of All of a Kind Family — Sydney Taylor
Henry and Mudge — Cynthia Rylant
Nate the Great — Marjorie Weinman
Hank the Cowdog — John R. Erikson
Golly Sisters series — Betsy Byars
The King of Thing — Steve and Megan Scheibner
Frog and Toad series — Arnold Lobel
Danger at the Breaker — Catherine Welch
Keep the Lights Burning, Abbie — Peter and Connie Roop
The Courage of Sarah Noble — Alice Dalgliesh
Sarah Plain and Tall — Patricia MacLachlan
George and Martha — James Marshall
Amelia Bedelia — Herman Parish
Baby — Patricia MacLachlan
The Bears on Hemlock Mountain — Alice Dalgliesh
Mrs. Piggle — Wiggle — Betty MacDonald
Baby Island — Carol Ryrie Brink
Mice of the Nine Lives — Tim Davis
Mice of the Herring Bone — Tim Davis
Mice of the Seven Seas — Tim Davis
Mice of the Westing Wind — Tim Davis
Captive Treasure — Milly Howard
The Bridge — Jeri Massi
Crown and Jewel — Jeri Massi

The Two Collars — Jeri Massi
Understood Betsy — Dorothy Canfield Fisher
With Daring Faith — Rebecca Davis
The Year of Jubilo — Ruth Sawyer
Thee, Hannah — Marguerite de Angeli
Henner's Lydia — Marguerite de Angeli
Copper — Toed Boots — Marguerite de Angeli
Petite Suzanne — Marguerite de Angeli
Tom Swift series — copyrighted prior to 1971
Little House In the Big Woods — Laura Ingalls Wilder
Farmer Boy — Laura Ingalls Wilder
Little House on the Prairie — Laura Ingalls Wilder
On the Banks of Plum Creek — Laura Ingalls Wilder
By the Shores of Silver Lake — Laura Ingalls Wilder
The Long Winter — Laura Ingalls Wilder
Little Town on the Prairie — Laura Ingalls Wilder
These Happy Golden Years — Laura Ingalls Wilder
Black Beauty — Anna Sewall
The Black Stallion — Walter Farley
The Black Stallion Returns — Walter Farley
Misty of Chincoteague — Marguerite Henry
Justin Morgan Had a Horse — Marguerite Henry
King of the Wind — Marguerite Henry
Sea Star, Orphan of Chincoteague — Marguerite Henry
Born to Trot — Marguerite Henry
Brighty of the Grand Canyon — Marguerite Henry
Stormy, Misty's Foal — Marguerite Henry
White Stallion of Lipizza — Marguerite Henry
Misty's Twilight — Marguerite Henry
The Lion, the Witch, and the Wardrobe — C.S. Lewis
Prince Caspian — C.S. Lewis

The Voyage of the Dawn Treader — C.S. Lewis

The Silver Chair — C.S. Lewis

The Horse and His Boy — C.S. Lewis

The Magician's Nephew — C.S. Lewis

The Last Battle — C.S. Lewis

Farmer Giles of Ham — J.R.R. Tolkien

## Older Readers:

The Wind in the Willows — Kenneth Grahame

Lost on a Mountain In Maine — Donn Fendler

Island of the Blue Dolphins — Scott O'Dell

Elsie Dinsmore series — Martha Finley

Johnny Tremain — Esther Forbes

Dust of the Earth — Donna Hess

The Lost Prince — Frances Hodgson Burnett

Robinson Crusoe — Daniel Defoe

Apples To Oregon — Deborah Hopkinson and Mary Carpenter

A Little Princess — Frances Hodgson Burnett

Hans Brinker and the Silver Skates — Mary Maples Dodge

Calico Bush — Rachel Field

Carry On Mr. Bowditch — Jean Lee Latham

Eight Cousins — Louisa May Alcott

Rose In Bloom — Louisa May Alcott

Little Women — Louisa May Alcott

Little Men — Louisa May Alcott

Under the Lilacs — Louisa May Alcott

An Old Fashioned Girl — Louisa May Alcott

The Hobbit — J.R.R. Tolkien

The Fellowship of the Ring — J.R.R. Tolkien

The Two Towers — J.R.R. Tolkien

The Return of the King — J.R.R. Tolkien

Treasures of the Snow  — Patricia St. John

Star of Light  —  Patricia St. John

The Tanglewoods' Secret  —  Patricia St. John

Rainbow Garden  —  Patricia St. John

Anne of Green Gables  — Lucy Maude Montgomery

Anne of the Island  — Lucy Maude Montgomery

Anne of Avonlea  — Lucy Maude Montgomery

Anne's House of Dreams  —  Lucy Maude Montgomery

Rainbow Valley  —  Lucy Maude Montgomery

Roll of Thunder Hear My Cry  — Mildred D. Taylor

Big Red  — Jim Kjelgaard

Snow Dog  —  Jim Kjelgaard

Irish Red, Son of Big Red  —  Jim Kjelgaard

Outlaw Red, Son of Big Red  —  Jim Kjelgaard

Desert Dog  —  Jim Kjelgaard

Tom Sawyer  — Mark Twain

A Girl of the Limberlost  — Gene Stratton Porter

Freckles  — Gene Stratton Porter

The Harvester  — Gene Stratton Porter

Not My Will  — Fancena H. Arnold

Stepping Heavenward  — Elizabeth Prentiss

The Count of Monte Cristo  — Alexandre Dumas

Ben Hur  — Lew Wallace

Emma  — Jane Austen

Drums  — James Boyd

Treasure Island  —  Robert Louis Stevenson

A Tale of Two Cities  — Charles Dickens

20,000 Leagues Under the Sea  — Jules Verne

The Mysterious Island  — Jules Verne

Scottish Chiefs  — Jane Porter

The Swiss Family Robinson  — Johann Wyss

Robinson Crusoe –Daniel Defoe

Peter Pan –J.M. Barrie

The Kings Swift Rider –Mollie Hunter

The Black Arrow –Robert Louis Stevenson

Pilgrims Progress –John Bunyan

Last of the Mohicans — James Fenimore Cooper

The Adventures of Sherlock Holmes — Sir Arthur Conan Doyle

Les Miserable–Victor Hugo

The Hunchback of Notre Dame — Victor Hugo

Moby Dick — Herman Melville

Ivanhoe — Sir Walter Scott

The Strange Case of Dr. Jekyll and Mr. Hyde
    — Robert Louis Stevenson

Kidnapped — Robert Louis Stevenson

Around the World in 80 Days — Jules Verne

Lorna Dorne — R.D. Blackmore

Jane Eyre — Charlotte Bronte

The Scarlet Letter — Nathaniel Hawthorne

The Odyssey — Homer

The Illiad — Homer

The Jungle Book — Rudyard Kipling

Red Badge of Courage — Stephen Crane

A Christmas Carol — Charles Dickens

Great Expectations — Charles Dickens

Arabian Knights — unknown

Man In the Iron Mask — Alexander Dumas

Frankenstein — Mary Shelley

A Connecticut Yankee in King Arthur's Court — Mark Twain

Time Machine — H.G. Wells

War of the Worlds — H.G.Wells

The Three Musketeer — Alexander Dumas

The Prince and the Pauper — Mark Twain
Roverandom — J.R.R. Tolkien
The Silmarillion — J.R.R. Tolkien
The Biography of Stonewall Jackson — James Robertson
All G.A. Henty books
Books in the Landmark history series
Making Home Happy — L.D. Avery — Stuttle

# BOOKS TO ENCOURAGE YOUR HEART
## AND INSPIRE YOUR IMAGINATION

Homeschooling With a Meek and Quiet Spirit — Teri Maxwell
Desiring God — John Piper
Don't Waste Your Life — John Piper
The Mission of Motherhood — Sally Clarkson
The Ministry of Motherhood — Sally Clarkson
Educating the Wholehearted Child — Sally Clarkson
Seasons of a Mother's Heart Sally Clarkson
Dancing With My Father — Sally Clarkson
The Mom Walk: Keeping in Step with God's Heart
    for Motherhood — Sally Clarkson
My Heart's at Home — Jill Savage
Discipline, The Glad Surrender — Elizabeth Elliot
The Shaping of a Christian Family — Elizabeth Elliot
The Fulfilled Family — John MacArthur
The Successful Christian Homeschool Family
    — Raymond and Dorothy Moore
What Is a Family — Edith Schaeffer
The Most Important Place on Earth — Robert Wolgemuth
The Mentoring Mom — Jackie Kendall
First We Have Coffee — Margaret Jenson

Reaping the Harvest: The Bounty of Abundant
   — Life Homeschooling — Diana Waring
Beyond Survival: A Guide to Abundant Life Homeschooling
   — Diana Waring
Things We Wish We'd Known — compiled by Diana Waring
Homeschooling: A Patchwork of Days
   — compiled by Nancy Lande
Homeschool Open House — compiled by Nancy Lande
Romancing Your Child's Heart — Monte Swan
Hearth and Home: Recipes For Life — Karey Swan
Secret Keeper, The Delicate Power of Modesty
   — Dannah Gresh
The Purity Principle — Randy Alcorn
Looking At Myself Before Loving Someone Else
   — John Coblentz

## Internet Encouragement:

Aholyexperience.com — Ann Voskamp
Chattingatthesky — Emily Freeman
Pioneer Woman — Ree Drummond
Meganscheibner.com — Building Character/
   Making Memories (My blog)

## Sites For "Stuff"

Timberdoodle Company
Hearthsong
Rainbow Resource
Christian Book Distributors
Characterhealth.com

# AIDS FOR EDUCATIONAL ENDEAVORS

## Bible and Spiritual Life:

Egermeier's Bible Story Book — Elsie Egermeier
The Little Pilgrim's Progress — Helen Taylor
A Hive of Busy Bees — Effie Williams

## Language Arts:

Teach Your Child to Read in 100 Easy Lessons
Pathway Readers
Christian Liberty Press Readers
Explode the Code
The "Bob" Books
Wordly Wise
Easy Grammar
Apples: Daily Spelling Drills
Spellwell
Learning Language Arts Through Literature
Write Shop

## Handwriting:

A Reason For Writing
Ready Writer

## Mathematics:

BJU Mathematics
Keys To…math curriculum (fractions, decimals, geometry,
    measurement)
A Teaching Textbook Algebra I, Algebra II

## Science:

Apologia Resources:
Exploring Creation with Astronomy
Exploring Creation with Biology
Exploring Creation with Zoology
Exploring Creation with Human Anatomy and Physiology
Exploring Creation with General Science
Exploring Creation with Physical Science
Exploring Creation with Biology
Exploring Creation with Chemistry
Human Body/Advanced Biology
Christian Liberty Nature Readers Books1 — 6
Magic School Bus Science Kits

## History and Geography:

Runkle Geography
Beautiful Feet Literature Approach to Geography
Beautiful Feet Literature Approach to Ancient History
Beautiful Feet Literature Approach to Medieval History
Beautiful Feet Literature Approach to Early American History
Westward Expansion: A Literature Approach
The Story of US
The Story of the World: History for the Classical Child

# Finding Time For Fun:

## Resources and Recreation

### Audio Resources:

Adventures In Odyssey
Your Story Hour
Focus on the Family Radio Theatre
 The Chronicles of Narnia
 Billy Bud; Sailor
 Les Miserables
 Father Gilbert Series
 The Screwtape Letters
 Amazing Grace
Jonathon Park Series
A Series of Unfortunate Events
The Lord of the Rings — BBC edition
Look for unabridged books on CD

### Video Resources:

Answers in Genesis
All Creatures Great and Small

## Games and Puzzles:

| | |
|---|---|
| Ravensburger Puzzles | White Mountain Puzzles |
| SET | Quiddler |
| Phase 10 | Checkers |
| Chess | Sequence |
| Into the Forest | Into the Desert |
| Mancala | Backgammon |
| Dominoes | Chinese Checkers |
| Monopoly | Trivial Pursuit |
| Clue | Risk |
| Dutch Blitz | Uno |
| Sort It Out | Sorry |
| Connect 4 | Hi – Ho Cherry – 0 |
| Scattergories | Bananagrams |
| Family Talk | Spot It |
| Life | Charades |
| Farkel | Yahtzee |
| Othello | Twister |
| Go – Fish | Skip – Bo |

# Study Guide

*Dear Reader,*

My prayer is that The A-Z Guide for Character Healthy Home-schooling has been an encouragement to your heart. However, I know that reading a book and actually retaining the information are two different things. With that in mind, the following Study Guide is designed to help you interact with the concepts presented in each of the chapters.

Designed for individual, or group use, the study guide utilizes discussion questions, Scripture look-ups, and practical applications to make The A-Z Guide an individualized learning experience. Associated memory verses will provide help and direction on those difficult homeschooling days!

For those of you who plan to use the study in a group session, I would encourage you to add personal examples to assist in incorporating such topics as: Knotty Situations, Attitudes, Delegating Chores, and more. The included questions are simply a jumping off point for more discussion and for building community within your group of homeschooling parents.

Have fun with the study! May God bless your efforts and remember... Don't Grow Weary of Doing Well!

In Christ,

*Megan Ann*

# ATTITUDE IS EVERYTHING

## Think About It:

In your home, what attitudes do you consider to be the most important?

_____

_____

_____

_____

What attitudes do you think characterize your family's testimony?
Do the two types of attitudes match?

_____

_____

_____

_____

_____

## Dig It Out:

Read Proverbs 17:22. What causes you to have joy on a daily basis? Is your joy based on your circumstances?

_____

_____

_____

_____

Look up the definition of circumstances. Is your level of joyfulness contingent on the daily up-and-down circumstances in your life? On what permanent truths can you base your joy?

_____

_____

_____

_____

## Make It Work:

Make a list of the "joy-robbers" that you face during a normal day. Consider what practical steps you can take to alleviate the stressful circumstances and the poor attitudes that these circumstances cause throughout your day. Consider what activities can be eliminated to safeguard your family's time and peacefulness. What tools can you use to help your children remember to have a good attitude?

_____

_____

_____

_____

_____

## Pray About It:

Spend time in prayer asking the Lord to clearly reveal what attitudes characterize you and your homeschooling.

Pray for guidance to make good choices in how you order your day, in order to eliminate those circumstances that elevate poor attitudes in your home.

## Make It Yours:

Memorize Proverbs 17:22

# BALANCE, BALANCE, BALANCE

## Think About It:

What are the positive benefits you experience when your life is in balance?

_____
_____
_____
_____
_____

Was there a time in your life when everything felt more balanced? When was that time?

_____
_____
_____
_____
_____

When your life is out of balance, how can you regain Biblical balance?

_____
_____
_____
_____
_____

## Dig It Out:

Read I Thessalonians 4:11. How do you define a quiet life?

_____
_____
_____
_____

Is it possible to care about and be involved in other's lives, while still "attending to your own business?"

_____

_____

In your own unique situation, what does it look like to "Work with your hands?"

_____

_____

_____

_____

_____

## Make It Work:

If you haven't already, make a list of your top five priorities.

_____

_____

_____

_____

_____

Considering that list, determine whether or not your priorities are well maintained. Carefully determine what activities tend to rob your home and homeschooling of their much-needed balance.

## Pray About It:

Pray and ask the Lord to affirm your list of priorities. Make sure that your list is actually His list. Seek God's forgiveness for the ways that you have allowed other things to steal time from your priorities.

## Make It Yours:

Memorize I Thessalonians 4:11. Review Proverbs 17:22.

# Contagious Excitement

## Think About It:

What makes you excited? Have you ever had to participate in something totally, "Uncool," in order to generate excitement in others? What was it that you had to do?

_____

_____

_____

_____

_____

## Dig It Out:

Read Psalm 47:1. What are two ways, according to this verse, that we can show excitement in our relationship with the Lord?

_____

_____

_____

_____

_____

In what outward ways do you exhibit excitement in your home and homeschooling?

_____

_____

_____

_____

_____

## Make It Work:

Today, determine to overflow with excitement in your tasks. At the end of the day, consider whether or not this overflowing excitement made a difference in your school day.

Sometimes, our actions are the building blocks necessary to develop a great attitude; excitement builds more excitement! When we are thankful, we will overflow with excitement-building joy. With your children, take the time to make a list of things for which you are thankful and add to that list daily.

## Pray About It:

Do you find it hard to generate excitement? Pray and ask the Lord to fill your heart with His joy and excitement.

Pray, thanking God for all the blessings and protections He brings into your life.

Pray that your children would see the joy that resides in your heart.

## Make It Yours:

Memorize Psalm 47:1. Review Proverbs 17:22 and I Thessalonians 4:11.

# DESIGNATE CHORES AND CHORE TIME

## Think About It:

Do you delegate to others, or do you feel as though you must do everything by yourself?

_____

_____

_____

_____

What lessons do your children learn as they participate in family duties?

_____

_____

_____

_____

## Dig It Out:

Read Exodus 18:18. Who would be worn out if Moses continued to carry on his normal routine?

_____

_____

_____

Jethro didn't say that Moses' counsel to the people was wrong, or poorly executed; rather, what was the problem?

_____

_____

_____

What tasks do you carry that are too heavy for you?

_____

_____

_____

_____

_____

## Make It Work:

Do you have an adequate and workable chore system?

_____

_____

_____

_____

_____

Make a list of the necessary daily chores that must be accomplished in order for your home to run smoothly.

_____

_____

_____

_____

Take time to designate chores to your children. Train each child in the proper execution of those chores. Praise your children for chores that are well done!

## Pray About It:

Ask the Lord to clearly show you what areas you can safely delegate to others.

Thank the Lord for the rest He provides as you lighten your load by delegation.

Pray for your children as they grow in responsibility.

## Make It Yours:

Memorize Exodus 18:18. Review Proverbs 17:22, I Thessalonians 4:11, and Psalm 47:1.

# EXPECTATIONS:
## NEVER WORTH THE TROUBLE THEY CAUSE

## Think About It:

What is the difference between an expectation and a standard?

_____

_____

_____

_____

_____

Why do you think that expectations cause such strife?

_____

_____

_____

_____

## Dig It Out:

Read Proverbs 13:10. What are some areas of expectation – "presumption" – that cause strife in your home?

_____

_____

_____

Do certain situations prompt more expectations to pop up unexpectedly?

_____

_____

_____

## Make It Work:

Consider what areas of your family life are experiencing strife. Can you recognize any expectations that you are bringing to those areas?

_____

_____

_____

_____

Determine what standards are necessary for your home to function in a healthy manner. Clearly communicate those standards. Discard any expectations, and as necessary, seek forgiveness for imposing your expectations on others.

## Pray About It:

Seek God and ask Him to reveal any expectations you are bringing into your homeschooling day.

Seek His forgiveness for the strife you promote in your home

Pray and ask God to help you to develop Biblical standards and discard unfruitful expectations.

## Make It Yours:

Memorize Proverbs 13:10. Review all previous memorized verses.

# FUN TIMES

## Think About It:

What are your favorite fun times?

_____

_____

_____

_____

_____

What are your favorite, "Fun time," memories from your own childhood?

_____

_____

_____

_____

_____

Have you incorporated those memories with your own family?

_____

_____

_____

_____

## Dig It Out:

Read Ecclesiastes 3:1. How can you make time to include fun in your family's daily routine?

_____

_____

_____

_____

Do you think that God considers fun to be necessary? Why or why not?

_____

_____

_____

_____

What are some different seasons of life for you and how do those seasons change your family dynamic?

_____

_____

_____

_____

## Make It Work:

Make a list of five fun activities, (One for each school day this week). Choose one activity and make it happen, each day.

_____

_____

_____

_____

_____

Ask your children to help you to construct a Master List of, "Things We'd Like To Do". Nothing is too crazy to go on this list! With calendar in hand, plan some of these activities into your busy schedule.

## Pray About It:

Pray and ask God to help you overcome any obstacles to having fun with your family.
Pray for His imagination to help you create fun memories.

## Make It Yours:

Memorize Ecclesiastes 3:1. Review all previously memorized verses.

# GET ORGANIZED

## Think About It:

Did you grow up in an organized home?

_____

_____

_____

How does organization, or a lack thereof, affect the attitudes and actions in your home?

_____

_____

_____

_____

What areas of orderliness are most important to you?

_____

_____

_____

_____

## Dig It Out:

Read I Corinthians 14:40. What areas of your life constitute the, "All things," that must be orderly?

_____

_____

_____

_____

Can our own minds be held to an attitude of decency and order?

_____

_____

_____

_____

How can we discipline our minds to function in an orderly way?

_____

_____

_____

_____

## Make It Work:

Evaluate your home. What areas need to be organized in a more orderly manner? Make a list of needed changes and develop a plan to successfully organize those areas.

Enlist your family's help. Ask your husband and/or children what areas are frustrating to them and develop a strategic plan to help your home function in a decent and orderly manner.

## Pray About It:

Ask God for the strength to make changes.

Pray for clarity to make appropriate changes that will glorify God and strengthen your testimony

## Make It Yours:

Memorize I Corinthians 14:40. Review all previously memorized verses.

# Hovering Hinders

## Think About It:

Do you hover? It is almost impossible to self-evaluate our own hovering. Ask your husband, children, or a trusted friend to evaluate your level of hovering and/or over-involvement.

_____

_____

_____

_____

_____

## Dig It Out:

Read John 2:3-4. Do you think it was hard for Mary to allow Jesus to venture into His own ministry?

_____

_____

_____

_____

_____

Read Matthew 20:20-21. Why do you think the mother of the Sons of Zebedee made her special request?

_____

_____

_____

_____

_____

## Make It Work:

This is a hard one: Make a list of the areas that cause you to hover. Look for common attributes in those areas. Do you hover when you are fearful of physical harm? Or, perhaps, do you hover to make sure that your children get their, "Fair share"?

_____

_____

_____

_____

_____

Purposefully force yourself to step back and allow your children to learn the lessons that are afforded to them by these trying circumstances.

## Pray About It:

Pray for the self-control to stop hovering

Ask God to help you hate any areas of over-control that you exhibit.

## Make It Yours:

Memorize John 2:3-4. Review all previously memorized verses.

# INFUSE YOUR HOMESCHOOL WITH PRAYER

## Think About It:

When are your best times of prayer?

_____
_____
_____
_____
_____

What recent answers to prayer have you received?

_____
_____
_____
_____

How has prayer strengthened your relationship with the Lord?

_____
_____
_____
_____

## Dig It Out:

Read I Thessalonians 5:17. Using a concordance, make a list of verses concerning prayer.

_____
_____
_____
_____
_____

Record the verses that you find to be the most encouraging and tape or hang them in a prominent place.

_____

_____

_____

_____

_____

## Make It Work:

Prayer takes commitment. Without a plan, prayer will often become random or haphazard. Purchase a small notebook and record your prayer requests. When those prayers are answered, record the answer in your notebook. I find it helpful to date God's answers to my prayers. When I'm discouraged, looking back at those answers provides great encouragement.

## Pray About It:

Pray! Just do it! Make it a practice to seek God consistently and persistently throughout your day. Remember to stop and pray with your children to bring God's presence into their problems and distresses.

## Make It Yours:

Memorize I Thessalonians 5:17. Review all previously memorized verses.

# JUST THE MEANS TO AN END

## Think About It:

What goals and dreams did you have as a child?

_____

_____

_____

_____

_____

Did your parents help you to reach those goals?

_____

_____

_____

_____

_____

How do those past goals fit into your present life?

_____

_____

_____

_____

_____

## Dig It Out:

Read I Corinthians 10:31. Is it possible to glorify God in all that we do?

_____

_____

_____

_____

_____

Why do you think God chose eating and drinking, two mundane activities, as His template for exhibiting His glory?

_____

_____

_____

_____

_____

## Make It Work:

Do you know what your children's dreams for the future include? If not, spend time dreaming out loud with them and helping them to formalize their goals. Ask them what you can do to help them reach their goals. Encourage them to try new and varied activities in order to make informed decisions about their future. Share some of the dreams you have for their future with them and spend time dialoging about those dreams.

## Pray About It:

Pray for each of your children individually.

Pray that God would help them to discern His will for their lives. Remember, it's never too early to pray for their future spouses.

## Make It Yours:

Memorize I Corinthians 10:31. Review all previously memorized verses.

# Knotty Situations

Think About It:

What people have truly encouraged you about your decision to home-school?

_____

_____

_____

_____

_____


How did they encourage you?

_____

_____

_____

_____

_____


Do family members respect your decision?

_____

_____

_____

_____


## Dig It Out:

Read James 1:2-3. In these verses, the word "various" literally means "multi-colored." What multi-colored trials have you encountered in your homeschooling?

_____

_____

_____

_____

Have those trials produced joy in your life?

_____

_____

_____

_____

_____

Practically speaking, how can we find joy when circumstances are difficult?

_____

_____

_____

_____

_____

## Make It Work:

Knotty situations are difficult to handle. Plan ahead of time how you will respond to those who criticize you, your family, or your decision to homeschool. Take some time to instruct your children about how they should respond to criticism. Remember, a gentle answer turns away wrath (Proverbs 15:1). As a family, purpose to allow God to be your defender.

## Pray About It:

Pray for a loving attitude toward those who criticize you.

Pray that God would develop in your family a winsome testimony that draws others to Him.

## Make It Yours:

Memorize James 1:2-3. Review all previously memorized verses.

# Learn to Love the Basics

## Think About It:

What was your favorite subject in school?

_____
_____
_____
_____

What was your least favorite subject?

_____
_____
_____
_____

Do you have more fun teaching certain subjects to your children? What are those subjects?

_____
_____
_____
_____

## Dig It Out:

Read Isaiah 28:10. In your spiritual life, what are the basics that must be built upon step by step?

_____
_____
_____
_____

Evaluate your children's spiritual lives. Have they spent adequate time learning the basics of the faith?

_____

_____

_____

_____

_____

Can they appropriately defend their faith? Can you?

_____

_____

_____

_____

_____

## Make It Work:

If you, or your children, need a refresher in the basics of the faith, make a priority plan to fill this need. Spend time together completing a basic discipleship study, (I.e. Bible Basics, available at Characterhealth.com). Spend time reviewing academic and social basics, as well. Look for gaps in your children's development and find resources to fill those gaps.

## Pray About It:

Ask God to show you any, "Gap-type" needs in your children's lives. Pray for the consistency necessary to do the hard work of mastering the basics.

## Make It Yours:

Memorize Isaiah 28:10. Review all previously memorized verses.

# MAKE THE MOST OF LEARNING STYLES

## Think About It:

How do you most easily acquire information?

_____
_____
_____
_____
_____

Is there a certain way of learning that seems impossible to you?

_____
_____
_____
_____

Do you think that most curriculums cater to a certain learning style? Which style?

_____
_____
_____
_____
_____

## Dig It Out:

Read I Corinthians 12:17. Why is it important to recognize our children's learning styles?

_____
_____
_____
_____

Is one learning style more important, or acceptable, than another?

_____

_____

_____

_____

How can you help your children begin to learn in a style that is not natural for them?

_____

_____

_____

_____

_____

## Make It Work:

Carefully consider your homeschooling resources. Do you have adequate supplies to address all of the unique learning styles your children possess?

_____

_____

_____

Take some time to dialogue with your children, asking them to explain how it is easiest for them to learn. Encourage your children to develop all three learning styles and praise them when they show good effort.

## Pray About It:

Pray for patience in teaching to those learning styles that are not compatible with your own.
Pray for creativity as you meet your children's educational needs.

## Make It Yours:

Memorize I Corinthians 12:17. Review all previously memorized verses.

# No Curriculum Does it All

## Think About It:

What's the first question you ask other homeschoolers?

_____

_____

_____

How did you choose your curriculum?

_____

_____

_____

_____

What's your favorite homeschooling resource?

_____

_____

_____

_____

## Dig It Out:

Read Proverbs 4:7. What is the difference between wisdom and knowledge?

_____

_____

_____

_____

Considering your chosen homeschool resources, are you teaching to develop intellect, or character?

_____

_____

_____

Are you depending too much on your curriculum and neglecting to use your godly influence to develop your children's character?

_____

_____

_____

_____

## Make It Work:

How can you better utilize the curriculum resources you already own?

_____

_____

_____

_____

Don't be enslaved to your curriculum. Look through the work that you will be assigning to your children this week. Find a way to use that curriculum to assist your children in building strong moral muscle. As your school year progresses, take time to record what you like and dislike about the curriculum you are using. Refer back to these notes as you make decisions regarding the next school year.

## Pray About It:

Always pray for wisdom as you select curriculum.

Pray for the discernment to make decisions based on God's will for your family, not on the latest fad of the other sheep-like homeschooling parents.

## Make It Yours:

Memorize Proverbs 4:7. Review all previously memorized verses.

# OBSERVING RELATIONSHIPS

## Think About It:

If you had siblings, with which sibling did you enjoy the closest relationship? Why?

_____

_____

_____

_____

_____

How do you maintain that relationship now that you're older?

_____

_____

_____

_____

_____

## Dig It Out:

Read I John 4:11. What is the basis on which we can build our love for one another?

_____

_____

_____

_____

_____

Do we have a choice not to love one another?

_____

_____

_____

_____

_____

_____

Read I Corinthians 13. Why do you think love is the greatest gift?

_____

_____

_____

_____

_____

_____

## Make It Work:

Observe your family dynamics. Are there certain relationships that need to change in order to bring glory to God?

If so, help those involved in the relationship to make a workable plan to build and restore closeness within their relationship. (A helpful tool for building family relationships is found in the, "Loving Our Family Guidelines," contained in the Parenting Matters DVD set, available from Characterhealth.com.)

## Pray About It:

Pray for wisdom to help your children facilitate closeness and peacefulness in their relationships.
Pray for specific sibling pairings and the issues they face.

## Make It Yours:

Memorize I John 4:11. Review all previously memorized verses.

# Practicing God's Peace

## Think About It:

What circumstances rob you of peace?

_____

_____

_____

_____


Is your family characterized by an atmosphere of trust in God?

_____

_____

_____

_____


How can you show your children that God is trustworthy?

_____

_____

_____

_____


## Dig It Out:

Read Philippians 4:6-7. What should accompany our prayer and supplication?

_____

_____

_____

How can being thankful help us to be peaceful?

_____

_____

_____

_____

What will God's peace produce in your heart and mind?

_____

_____

_____

_____

_____

## Make It Work:

Again, let me encourage you to make an ongoing list of blessings for which you are thankful. As well, memorized Scripture pertaining to God's faithfulness is a powerful antidote to fear and worry. This week, when fear threatens to overwhelm your heart and mind, discipline yourself to instead: Stop, Thank God, and Pray!

## Pray About It:

Pray for the strength and discipline to hand your cares over to God.

Pray, asking God's help to bring memorized passages to mind when you need them the most.

## Make It Yours:

Memorize Philippians 4:6-7. Review all previously memorized verses.

# QUASHING CURVEBALLS

## Think About It:

How do you usually respond when God throws you a curveball?

_____

_____

_____

_____

_____

What is the latest curveball that God has thrown your way?

_____

_____

_____

_____

_____

What was the end result?

_____

_____

_____

_____

_____

## Dig It Out:

Read James 1:12. What will we receive if we persevere under trials?

_____

_____

_____

How can we remind ourselves of the end reward when we are in the midst of a present trial?

_____

_____

_____

Do you believe that God throws curveballs for our benefit? Why or why not?

_____

_____

_____

_____

## Make It Work:

Take some time to record some of the curveballs that God has thrown into your life.

_____

_____

_____

Consider how you reacted to those curveballs. Do you see any recurring patterns?

_____

_____

_____

As you notice negative patterns emerging, make a list of positive, proactive actions you can incorporate to better handle those curveball situations.

_____

_____

_____

## Pray About It:

Pray for the discernment to see and recognize curveballs before they catch you unaware.

Ask God to help you build the spiritual muscle necessary to successfully quash curveballs.

## Make It Yours:

Memorize James 1:12. Review all previously memorized verses.

# REST, READING, AND OTHER ROUTINE-BREAKERS

## Think About It:

Do you incorporate adequate rest time into your day? What happens when you over-worked in any area of your life?

_____

_____

_____

_____

_____

_____

What is your favorite way to find rest?

_____

_____

_____

_____

_____

## Dig It Out:

Read Matthew 11:28. What does Jesus promise to those who are weary and heavy laden?

_____

_____

_____

_____

_____

Is it always possible to notice when our family members are over-burdened?

_____

_____

_____

_____

_____

_____


How can regular rest and relaxation keep us from being overburdened?

_____

_____

_____

_____

_____

_____


## Make It Work:

Do your children struggle to take a rest time?

_____

_____

_____

_____

_____

_____


With their help, make a list of appropriate rest and relaxation activities. When they are stumped for ideas, refer them to the list. Reading is so important! Insist that your children spend time reading. Allow them to choose reading materials, but if they aren't able, (Or willing,) to choose on their own, be ready with a book of your choosing.

## Pray About It:

Ask God to help you to notice when your children need a work break!

Pray for discernment to notice the difference between when they need a break in their routine and when they just need to stick with their assigned tasks.

## Make It Yours:

Memorize Matthew 11:28. Review all previously memorized verses.

# Stop the Competition

## Think About It:

Think about recent television shows. How many of these shows are based on competition and pitting one person or group against another

_____

_____

_____

_____

_____

Why do you think so many of these shows have gained so much popularity?

_____

_____

_____

_____

_____

## Dig It Out:

Read Philippians 2:3. In our daily interactions, for whom are we to be most concerned?

_____

_____

_____

_____

_____

_____

What attitude is necessary to be able to regard others as more important than us?

_____

_____

_____

_____

_____

When we think of ourselves first, according to this verse, what two negative character qualities are being exhibited?

_____

_____

_____

_____

_____

## Make It Work:

Is your family competitive? There is a huge difference between healthy competition and self-centered opposition. Take the time to discuss these differences with your children. If you have been guilty of an overly competitive spirit, seek God's forgiveness, and if appropriate, the forgiveness of anyone you've wronged.

## Pray About It:

Ask God to help you to hate your overly competitive spirit.

Pray for His wisdom to discern who simply needs your words of encouragement and with whom it is safe to share your children's successes without seeming competitive.

## Make It Yours:

Memorize Philippians 2:3. Review all previously memorized verses.

# Teaching Into "Duh", Dawdling, and Other Delays

## Think About It:

What causes dawdling in your home?

_____
_____
_____
_____
_____
_____

Are certain children more prone to dawdling than others?

_____
_____
_____
_____

Were you a dawdler?

_____
_____
_____
_____

## Dig It Out:

Read Ephesians 4:32. What three character qualities are we commanded to show one another?

_____
_____
_____
_____

Is there anything you do that adds to the dawdling in your home?

_____

_____

_____

When God forgave you, was it because you deserved to be forgiven?

_____

_____

_____

_____

Must your children deserve forgiveness in order to be forgiven by you?

_____

_____

_____

_____

## Make It Work:

Make a practical list of ways that you can show kindness to your children.

_____

_____

_____

_____

When their dawdling frustrates you, refer back to this list to find encouragement and strength to extend kindness and tender-mercies toward them. Determine in what ways you are facilitating dawdling and take the necessary steps to eradicate those actions from your home.

## Pray About It:

Pray for a heart of tenderness and kindness toward your children.

Pray for the discernment to differentiate a tired child from a disobedient child.

## Make It Yours:

Memorize Ephesians 4:32. Review all previously memorized verses.

# UNIQUE TALENTS AND STRENGTHS

## Think About It:

What is your most unique talent or strength?

_____

_____

_____

_____

_____

_____

What unique talents and strengths are exhibited by the other members of your family?

_____

_____

_____

_____

_____

How has God used those various talents to enhance your family's testimony?

_____

_____

_____

_____

_____

## Dig It Out:

Read I Corinthians 12:11. What strengths or talents does God consider as the most important in the body of Christ? Does He show partiality?

_____

_____

_____

_____

_____

_____

Are there certain gifts in your family that seem to gain more public acclaim?

_____

_____

_____

_____

_____

How can you encourage those family members who have less publicly noticeable strengths and talents?

_____

_____

_____

_____

_____

## Make It Work:

Ask your children good questions to help them to recognize the areas in which God has uniquely gifted them. Spend time evaluating your family. Is there a good balance in your family between using gifts publicly, and privately serving behind the scenes?

_____

_____

_____

_____

_____

_____

Brainstorm together to develop a workable plan to use your family's unique gifts to grow and edify the body of Christ.

## Pray About It:

Ask the Lord to show you your personal strengths and talents.
Pray for opportunities to use your gifts to glorify God.

## Make It Yours:

Memorize I Corinthians 12:11. Review all other previously memorized verses.

# VALIUM ISN'T THE ANSWER

## Think About It:

What is your favorite part of the homeschooling day?

_____
_____
_____
_____
_____

Which part of the day is the hardest?

_____
_____
_____
_____
_____

How do you survive those predictably hard times?

_____
_____
_____
_____
_____

## Dig It Out:

Read Galatians 6:9. According to this verse, what must we not lose?

_____

_____

_____

_____

In order to not lose heart, we must recognize that the daily work we are accomplishing is GOOD! When we realize this fact, we can press on through diverse obstacles. Remember, in the end we will reap and that reaping will be blessings from God Himself.

## Make It Work:

Make a list of activities or times of the day that are particularly wearying. Spend some time considering how you can better deal with those times.

Perhaps you need to institute a rest hour for your children, or maybe outdoor play will help to burn off an over-abundance of energy. Being prepared when the wearying times come can be half the battle.

## Pray About It:

Pray for the strength to stand up under times of weariness.
Pray that God would help you to keep your eye on the goal: pleasing Him!

## Make It Yours:

Memorize Galatians 6:9. Review all other previously memorized verses.

# WE ALL LEARN TOGETHER

## Think About It:

Are you investing time to learn a new subject or hobby?

_____

_____

_____

_____

_____

What topics are exciting to you?

_____

_____

_____

_____

_____

Do you make time to delve deeply into your hobbies and interests?

_____

_____

_____

## Dig It Out:

Read I Peter 1:5-7. What nine character qualities are we to develop?

_____

_____

_____

_____

_____

Do you see these character qualities as a progression? Why or why not?

_____

_____

_____

_____

_____

_____

Will we ever be done learning about the Lord?

_____

_____

_____

_____

_____

## Make It Work:

Make a list of topics or activities that seem exciting to you.

_____

_____

_____

_____

_____

Go to the library and check out books on one of those topics. When your children are spending time reading, allot some time for you to read, as well. Make sure that you share what you are learning with your family. When appropriate, invite them to join you in learning about and experiencing new areas of interest.

## Pray About It:

Pray for an eager learner's heart.

Pray, asking God to open new avenues of discovery for you to follow.

## Make It Yours:

Memorize I Peter 1:5-7. Review all previously memorized verses.

# eXploration

## Think About It:

Do you like to spend time exploring?

_____
_____
_____
_____
_____
_____

What is your idea of the best type of exploration possible?

_____
_____
_____
_____
_____
_____

I would love to go on an archeological dig; what excites you?

_____
_____
_____
_____
_____
_____

## Dig It Out:

Read Psalm 139:14. What do we learn from this verse about God's works?

_____
_____
_____
_____
_____
_____

What attitude should the recognition of God's creativity invoke in our hearts?

_____
_____
_____
_____
_____
_____

How can you practically recognize God's works on a daily basis?

_____
_____
_____
_____
_____
_____

## Make It Work:

Take your children on an exploration trip. Whether it is through the woods, along the seashore, or up a mountain, spend time noticing, recording, and marveling in the mighty works of our God. Help your children to begin an ongoing nature workbook and provide opportunities for them to consistently add more information to their workbook.

## Pray About It:

Pray, as a family, prayers of thanksgiving for the amazing works of God. As you direct your prayers to Him, recite the specific God-breathed marvels which you encounter each day.

## Make It Yours:

Memorize Psalm 139:14. Review all previously memorized verses.

# "You're Not Fair"

## Think About It:

How do you try to make sure everything is, "Fair," in your home?

_____
_____
_____
_____
_____
_____

Do you believe that fairness is a necessity? Why or why not?

_____
_____
_____
_____
_____
_____

How do you deal with coveting?

_____
_____
_____
_____

## Dig It Out:

Read Deuteronomy 5:21. What did God recognize about His people and their character?

_____
_____
_____
_____

Because we all covet, does that make coveting acceptable?

_____

_____

_____

_____

Is coveting limited to children?

_____

_____

_____

_____

## Make It Work:

Consider areas that are covetous in your own life. Do you covet your neighbor's stuff? Your Pastor's family? Your best friend's vacation?

_____

_____

_____

_____

_____

_____

Our children don't necessarily learn coveting from us, but our example can have a strongly negative, or positive, impact on them. Call coveting what it is, (Sin,) and teach your children to be happy for one another.

## Pray About It:

Seek God's forgiveness for any areas of coveting in your own life.

Pray for discernment to realize when your children are coveting, and also, for the courage to deal with that coveting in an appropriate manner.

## Make It Yours:

Memorize Deuteronomy 5:21. Review all previously memorized verses.

# Zeroing In On Issues:
## The Family Conference Table

## Think About It:

How did your family resolve issues when you were growing up?

_____

_____

_____

_____

_____

_____

How do you resolve issues in your own home?

_____

_____

_____

_____

_____

_____

What happens when issues are left unresolved?

_____

_____

_____

_____

## Dig It Out:

Read James 1:19. According to this verse, what three actions are we commanded to take regarding others?

_____

_____

_____

_____

_____

Which of these three actions is the easiest to perform?

_____

_____

_____

_____

_____

Are all three actions necessary to Biblically deal with conflict? Why or why not?

_____

_____

_____

_____

_____

## Make It Work:

Do you have issues that need to be resolved within your family? Perhaps a family conference table can help to solve the issues in a peaceful and God-honoring manner. (To learn more about the family conference table, see the Parenting Matters DVD set, available from Characterhealth.com.) Unresolved issues will cause bitterness and continual strife, so take the necessary steps to work through any outstanding problems.

## Pray About It:

Pray for discernment to recognize any issues that are simmering beneath the surface in your home.

Pray that God would equip you to be a peacemaker.

## Make It Yours:

Memorize James 1:19. Review all previously memorized verses.

# About Megan Scheibner

Megan was born March 13th 1962 and came home to her adoptive family March 15th. She grew up in York, PA and graduated from York Suburban H.S. in 1980. Four years later, she earned a B.A. in Speech Communications from West Chester University. She uses her degree as she teaches and speaks at conferences and women's ministry functions, as well as in individual and couples counseling.

Megan is the home schooling mother of eight beautiful children, four boys and four girls. She has been married for 28 years to her college sweetheart, Steve Scheibner. Together they have co-authored Parenting Matters, The Nine Practices of the Pro-Active Parent. She is also the author of a series of discipleship books for mothers and several devotional Bible studies. Her latest book is titled "In My Seat," the story of Steve's 9/11 experience, which has captivated millions on YouTube.

Megan and Steve have a strong desire to equip today's parents to raise the next generation of character healthy leaders. In her spare time, she loves to run and play tennis. Megan enjoys writing, cooking, feeding teenagers, reading, and everything pertaining to the Boston Red Sox.

# Contact Us

Steve and Megan travel extensively facilitating parenting, marriage, and men's and women's conferences for churches and other organizations.

### Conferences available include:
- Parenting Matters
- Marriage Matters
- Character Matters
- Second Mile Leadership For Men
- The Wise Wife
- The A to Z of a Character Healthy Homeschool
- Woman to Woman: The Mentoring Model and more...

*To Speak with Steve or Megan please call:*
1-877-577-2736

*Or send them an email by clicking the* "Contact us" *tab at:*
Characterhealth.com

*Also, follow us on Twitter:*
@SteveScheibner
@MeganScheibner